Meno, Parmenides, and Theaetetus

THE BARNES & NOBLE LIBRARY OF ESSENTIAL READING

Meno, Parmenides, and Theaetetus

Plato

Translated by Benjamin Jowett

Introduction by Marc Lucht

Barnes & Noble
New York

THE BARNES & NOBLE
LIBRARY OF ESSENTIAL READING

Originally published circa 365 BCE

This 2008 edition published by Barnes & Noble, Inc.

Barnes & Noble, Inc.
122 Fifth Avenue
New York, NY 10011

ISBN-13: 978-1-4351-0786-1

Printed and bound in the United States of America

1 3 5 7 9 10 8 6 4 2

Contents

Introduction

It would be impossible to exaggerate the magnitude of Plato's influence on the trajectory of Western thought. Plato's ideas that reality is knowable and that truths about nature and morality are accessible primarily to rational thought, although controversial, provide even today the foundation for scientific and philosophical inquiry. His portrayal of a life devoted to intellectual inquiry and moral virtue has inspired and guided people for more than two millennia, and his depiction of education through dialogue established what is now called the "Socratic method," a set of pedagogical practices used in classrooms around the world. And Plato's exploration of the connection between liberty and the ability to think for oneself lies at the heart of modern views of citizenship, ethics, education, and the nature of individuality. Even 2,500 years after his death, his ideas are still being debated by scholars in the fields of ethics, theology, aesthetics, educational theory, political science, and the philosophy of science. The dialogues *Meno, Parmenides,* and *Theaetetus,* collected together in this volume, represent both Plato's early and later thinking, and show the progression of his ideas about education, reality, and the nature of the knowledge that discloses that reality to us. In addition to the importance of these dialogues for understanding the development of Plato's philosophical views, the *Meno* and *Theaetetus* are examples of his finest literary artistry, and the *Parmenides* is a paradigmatic example of purely conceptual metaphysical investigation.

Plato's real name was Aristocles. "Plato" was a nickname, meaning "broad," and may have referred to his stocky build. He was born in 427 BCE, either in Athens or Aegina. His family was aristocratic, and as a young man Plato had political ambitions. In 411, however, upon Athens' military defeat by Sparta and its allies in Sicily, an oligarchy composed in part by Plato's friends and relatives overthrew the democracy, and, as he observed their increasingly tyrannical conduct, Plato grew disillusioned with politics. When Plato was twenty-seven or twenty-eight, Socrates was executed, and along with other disciples of Socrates, Plato left Athens for nearby Megara, and soon traveled to southern Italy, Sicily, and perhaps Egypt. After his return to Athens, Plato founded the Academy in 387. Thought by some scholars to be the first university, the Academy soon became a major center of scholarship in philosophy, mathematics, political thought, astronomy, and natural history. Aristotle was a student there until Plato's death in 348 or 347, and the Academy endured until the first century BCE, when it closed over ideological controversy.

Plato's philosophical thinking was influenced by many of his predecessors, especially Parmenides and the Pythagoreans, but Socrates was his biggest inspiration and Plato saw him as the model for the philosophical life. Socrates was born around 470 BCE, and, as was Plato, in some ways was an Enlightenment figure, attacking religious obscurantism with a commitment to the rational pursuit of truth and justice. It is thought that Socrates was illiterate, and he left no books of his own. Most of what is known about him comes from Plato and Xenophon, both of whom wrote dialogues in which Socrates typically, though not always, is the central figure. Socrates was known as the gadfly of Athens, perpetually annoying other citizens with his attempts to get them to rationally demonstrate their opinions in conversation. Socrates claimed that his dialogues arose out of his attempt to test the oracle at Delphi's pronouncement that he was the wisest man alive. Thinking that she must have been mistaken, he engaged his fellow citizens in dialogue in the attempt to find someone who understood matters better than he, and what he famously discovered is the basis of what has come to be known as Socratic ignorance. Discussion with others reveals that whereas they hold many opinions, they are unable to justify them. Thus the reason Socrates was wiser than everyone else is that he was the only one aware of his own ignorance: the only thing he knew was that he knew nothing. Socrates personified a life devoted to intellectual inquiry pursued through a conversation that dismantles naïvely held certainties and resists dogmatic appeals to faith, authority, and superstition by constantly demanding rational justification of beliefs. The twentieth-century philosopher Karl Jaspers argued that Socrates, along with Confucius, Jesus, and the Buddha, was one of the four most influential individuals in history. Jaspers remarked that the joint pursuit of truth through dialogue was the fundamental fact of Socrates' life, and said that Socrates "conversed with artisans, statesmen, artists, Sophists, harlots . . . [for dialogue] is necessary for the truth itself, which by its very nature opens up to an individual only in dialogue with another individual. . . . [Socrates thereby enabled his fellow citizens] to discover the difficulties in the seemingly self-evident; he confused them, forced them to think, to search, to inquire over and over again. . . ."[1] Yet Socrates' relentless skepticism about received views and established authorities was seen as threatening. In 399, he was tried and executed on charges of impiety and corrupting the youth, solidifying his position in history as a martyr for virtue and the rational pursuit of truth—wherever it leads.

The majority of Plato's texts are written as dialogues. The dialogue form offers pleasures and presents challenges unique to the genre. One of the advantages of the dialogue over literary forms such as the essay is that the dialogue enables Plato not merely to tell his readers what he takes the philosophical life to be, but to show us through literary portraits of philosophers such as Socrates and dramatic representations of actual philosophical activity. The dramatic elements of the dialogues enable Plato to contextualize the discussions, and he employs foreshadowing, dramatic irony, and other literary techniques to enrich the reader's encounter with the ideas at play in the texts. Thus, for instance, the conversation in the *Meno* occurs shortly before Socrates' trial, and Anytus' warning to Socrates at line 94e that he should tread carefully when venturing to criticize the knowledge of virtue possessed by prominent Athenians should be seen against this background; indeed, Anytus would be one of Socrates' accusers at trial. Plato in this way raises the discussion's stakes, indicating that the dialogue's question about whether virtue can be taught is not just an abstract matter divorced from everyday life, but bears upon the most serious matters of life and death: Socrates' failure to teach virtue (or perhaps the Athenians' failure to learn from that teaching) resulted in his own death. What appears at first to be a relatively lighthearted discussion between Socrates and Meno, then, emerges against the background of a dramatic context of tragedy and dread. To take another example, the fact that in the *Parmenides* Plato presents a *young* Socrates engaging in philosophical discussion with—and being corrected by—the older and venerable philosopher Parmenides suggests that Plato is using the dialogue to criticize a theory as yet immature or insufficiently worked out. The view young Socrates defends is very much like the position Plato has the character of (mature) Socrates advocate in earlier dialogues such as the *Meno*; the *Parmenides* therefore consists of Plato's own critique of his earlier theories. What is more, choosing to present his analyses of philosophical ideas as dialogues among richly drawn literary characters enables Plato to reveal the rootedness of certain ideas in specific personality types, thereby permitting him to expose the dangers posed by philosophical positions that are motivated by self-righteousness and ambition for power.

The dialogue form also presents the reader with a distinctive kind of challenge, namely, that of figuring out exactly what Plato's own views are. Although he had been present for many of the historical Socrates' conversations, Plato never incorporated himself as a character into his dialogues. Thus there are no philosophical claims or arguments presented in Plato's own voice. Just because Socrates (or some other character) says something does not mean that Plato himself endorses it—especially as Socrates often seems to be speaking ironically, articulating the consequences of his interlocutors' mistaken views. One of the great strengths of the dialogue form is that its indeterminacy invites the reader to imagine himself or herself as part of the conversation. There are actually two concurrent dialogues, one between Socrates and his interlocutors, and one between the text and the reader. In fact, many dialogues, including the *Meno* and *Theaetetus*, end with no final solutions presented to answer the questions under consideration, thereby leaving the reader with the task of thinking through further the problems under consideration.

Particularly noteworthy about Plato's dialogues is their literary artistry. Indeed, the *Meno* and *Theaetetus* contain some of Plato's most vivid images: the image of memory as an aviary, that of Socrates as a torpedo fish or electric ray that paralyzes its victims, and that of Socrates as a midwife, himself barren or ignorant but possessing the ability to help others give birth to their own ideas. More generally, over the course of what often prove to be very complex philosophical investigations, Plato in his dialogues brings his characters alive with wit, sympathy, and sometimes ridicule. Indeed, he portrays Socrates so vividly that many readers feel as if they know him and as if they are party to his conversations. Plato's Socrates is so familiar to us, and the ideas at play in the dialogues are so interwoven with our understandings of ourselves and the world, that the great American philosopher Ralph Waldo Emerson was able to write:

> Plato is philosophy, and philosophy, Plato—at once the glory and the shame of mankind, since neither Saxon nor Roman have availed

> to add to any of his categories. No wife, no children had he, and the thinkers of all civilized nations are his posterity and are tinged with his mind. . . . Christianity is in it. Mahometanism draws all its philosophy . . . from him. Mysticism finds in Plato all its texts. . . . An Englishman reads and says, "how English!" a German—"how Teutonic!" an Italian—"how Roman and how Greek!" As they say that Helen of Argos had that universal beauty that everybody felt related to her, so Plato seems to a reader in New England an American genius. His broad humanity transcends all sectional lines.[2]

Bringing the *Meno, Parmenides,* and *Theaetetus* together in a single volume enables the reader to chart what is probably the most important development in Plato's thinking: the shift in his views of the relationship between the ideal forms and the physical world, and the resulting development in his attitude toward nature. Plato's theory of forms may at first seem mystifying to modern readers, yet because of the enduring influence of Plato's idea that reality is accessible primarily not to sensation but to reason and its abstract concepts, it stands as the cornerstone of Western thought. (In fact, the theory of the forms still orients the investigations of the natural sciences, insofar as science attempts to penetrate beneath the flux of sense experience to isolate unchanging laws and constants in terms of which change must be understood.) The theory of forms originates in Plato's abiding conviction that eternal and unchanging realities exist unaltered by the constant flux or unceasing dynamism of the sensible world. The forms, or ideas, as the Greek εἱδος (*eidos*) sometimes is translated, are the eternal essences or archetypes after which all objects of sense are patterned. As perfect and eternal, however, the forms cannot exist in space or time, for everything in the world of space and time is subject to change and decay. Thus all entities we encounter in our ordinary lives are imperfect and transient copies of transcendent ideals. Plato therefore held that the essences of things exist independently of those things, and these ideals are accessible not to sensation but to reason (and perhaps also to mystical intuition). He thought, too, that the forms are more fully real than their less perfect copies (much as we might say that a plastic apple is not a "real" apple because it fails to measure up to the ideal), and, as more fully real, are more properly objects of knowledge than are sensed things. Yet the forms do not include only the archetypes of physical objects. Plato is much more interested in the essences of beauty, justice, and goodness. One of his most important contributions to

Western thought is the idea that, since all beings are oriented toward the form of the good, human beings can aspire to know and live according to objective and unchanging moral standards that are woven into the very structure of reality itself.

At the time of *Meno,* according to prevailing views of the development of his work, Plato seems to have thought that since the transcendent forms were the appropriate objects of knowledge and aspiration, the natural world and our earthly lives are comparatively worthless. In his *Republic,* for instance, Socrates claims that since philosophers are "in love with that learning which discloses to them something of the being that *is* always," they would "forsake those pleasures that come through the body." He asks, "To an understanding endowed with magnificence and the contemplation of all time and being, do you think it possible that human life seem anything great?"[3] In the dialogue *Phaedrus,* Socrates remarks that nature has nothing to teach him. As the forms are transcendent, the source of all value, meaning, and truth is found only external to nature. Critics of Western culture such as Friedrich Nietzsche have seen this apparent devaluation of nature as symptomatic of an exceedingly dangerous form of decadence. Nietzsche argued that Christianity inherited this Platonic devaluation of the world (as seen, for instance, in its frequent condemnation of sensuality and "worldliness" in favor of supposedly eternal and purely spiritual rewards, and in its placing the divine in a transcendent heaven), and because of its baleful influence Western culture has incorporated and been corrupted by what he calls life-denying values. Nietzsche says that the metaphysical "concepts 'beyond' and 'true world' were invented in order to depreciate the only world that exists," and that, because of its orientation toward the transcendent and the allegedly "spiritual," in Christianity "anti-nature itself received the highest honors as morality and as law. . . ."[4] Christianity rendered Platonic thinking accessible to the masses, and its influence culminates in a decadent denigration of the body and a resignation from life and earthly goals. For Nietzsche, the struggle against Christianity is at its core a struggle against Plato.

Plato's *Parmenides* consists to a large extent in a painstaking and highly abstract critique of the "two worlds" conception of the relationship between the forms and the world, that is, the view elaborated in the earlier dialogues of the forms as transcendent, existing above a subordinate and less valuable earthly existence. (In fact, the intensity of its focus on this conceptual analysis leads Plato to drop the usual dramatic elements.) Because of its conceptual abstraction, it may be the dialogue that has been subject to the widest variety of interpretations. Some scholars have claimed, for instance, that it consists in a series of objections that prove fatal to Plato's earlier doctrine of forms and that he then abandons that theory; others have claimed that the dialogue demonstrates that Plato came to think his earlier theory was in need of revision. What is clear, however, is that the *Parmenides* constitutes a crucial transition in Plato's thought. Not only does the dialogue refute the idea that the forms must be wholly separate from the spatio-temporal world—a view frequently expressed in the dialogues written before the *Parmenides*, and here defended by a youthful Socrates in his conversation with the older Parmenides—but it makes clear that Plato anticipated critiques of the theory of forms along the lines of Nietzsche's. Thus, for instance, the character of young Socrates errs by supposing that physical and allegedly valueless things such as mud, hair, and dirt are unworthy of being patterned after forms. Plato recognizes that the view that the ideal is separate from the physical world results in an unacceptable denigration of nature, and the character of Parmenides uses young Socrates' error as a springboard from which to launch into a refutation of the conception of the absolute transcendence of the forms. In fact, as Mitchell Miller shows in his particularly lucid discussion of the *Parmenides*, Plato in this dialogue demonstrates that the forms must be both transcendent and immanent simultaneously; the forms must be both external to and integrated within the natural world. Nature accordingly must be regarded as containing the ideal within it.[5]

The *Parmenides* therefore marks a pivotal reorientation of the stance toward the natural world expressed in the earlier dialogues. Whereas earlier Plato seems uninterested in trying to understand the natural world, after the *Parmenides* Plato even turns his attention to cosmology and physiology. The *Theaetetus*, which most likely was written immediately after the *Parmenides*, is structurally similar to early dialogues such as the *Meno*, and consists in an exploration of the nature of knowledge, as does the *Meno*, but its approach recognizes the renewed interest in things of nature prepared for by the analysis of the *Parmenides*. Unlike the *Republic*, for instance, in which Socrates denies that knowledge of the natural world is even possible, the *Theaetetus* includes a thorough consideration of the relationship between knowledge and sensory perception, and prepares the way for an understanding of the conditions for knowledge even of natural phenomena. Considered artistically, the *Theaetetus* may be Plato's most masterfully composed dialogue, and it remains one of the most skillful philosophical analyses of the nature of knowledge in the history of ideas. What becomes clear over the course of the dialogue is that knowledge is not just the "neutral" apprehension of facts, but that understanding the nature of knowledge requires first understanding the limits and capacities of human intellect, and that genuine knowledge is tied inseparably to the resolve and moral character of the inquirer.

Plato's works are fascinating for the light they cast into antiquity, illuminating a remote world and culture that in many ways contained the seeds of our own. Yet more than this, at a time when the idea of objective moral standards is under attack and education increasingly is regarded as the mere transmission of information, Plato deserves to be read with renewed urgency. The three dialogues here include some of Plato's most characteristic portrayals of educational practice, and provide the reader with an overview of the evolution of his thinking about those ideas at the core of his philosophy: the nature of reality and knowledge.

Marc Lucht holds a Ph.D. in philosophy from Emory University. He has taught at Kenyon College, the University of Maine, and Rocky Mountain College and is now Assistant Professor of Philosophy at Alvernia College. He writes frequently on the history of modern philosophy, continental philosophy, aesthetics, and environmental ethics.

Editor's Note

The numeric marginalia found within this text are Stephanus numbering. In 1578, Henri Estienne, commonly known by the Latin name Stephanus, assembled an edition of Plato's dialogues that became the standard for scholars. Due to translation variances and reordering of the text, the numeric marginalia of this Barnes & Noble edition, like many modern editions, are not necessarily chronological. The Stepahnus numbers in the margin therefore assist in standardizing the way scholars refer to Plato's original, Greek text.

This edition includes two sets of notes: endnotes for the compendium as a whole and an appendix specific to *Meno*. Endnotes are indicated by Arabic numeral ascenders within the body of the text and will be found at the back of the book. The explanatory diagrams for *Meno* appear in the appendix. These notes are indicated by symbol ascenders within the body of the text. The diagrams and supporting text are found following the text of *Meno*, as indicated by the table of contents.

Meno

Meno

Characters of the Dialogue

Meno	A Slave of Meno
Socrates	Anytus

Meno. Can you tell me, Socrates, whether virtue is acquired by teaching or by practice; or if neither by teaching nor practice, then whether it comes to man by nature, or in what other way? 70a

Socrates. O Meno, there was a time when the Thessalians were famous among the other Hellenes only for their riches and their riding; but now, if I am not mistaken, they are equally famous for their wisdom, especially at Larissa, which is the native city of your friend Aristippus. And this is Gorgias' doing; for when he came there, the flower of the Aleuadae, among them your admirer Aristippus, and the other chiefs
of the Thessalians, fell in love with his wisdom. And he has taught you b
the habit of answering questions in a grand and bold style, which
becomes those who know, and is the style in which he himself answers c
all comers; and any Hellene who likes may ask him anything. How different is our lot! My dear Meno. Here at Athens, there is a dearth of
the commodity, and all wisdom seems to have emigrated from us to 71a
you. I am certain that if you were to ask any Athenian whether virtue was natural or acquired, he would laugh in your face and say: "Stranger, you have far too good an opinion of me if you think that I can answer your question. For I literally do not know what virtue is, and much less whether it is acquired by teaching or not." And I myself,
Meno, living as I do in this region of poverty, am as poor as the rest of b
the world, and I confess with shame that I know literally nothing about virtue; and when I do not know the "*quid*" of anything, how can I know

the "*quale*"? How, if I knew nothing at all of Meno, could I tell if he was fair or the opposite of fair; rich and noble, or the reverse of rich and noble? Do you think that I could?

c *MEN.* No, indeed. But are you in earnest, Socrates, in saying that you do not know what virtue is? And am I to carry back this report of you to Thessaly?

SOC. Not only that, my dear boy, but you may say further that I have never known of anyone else who did, in my judgment.

MEN. Then you have never met Gorgias when he was at Athens?

SOC. Yes, I have.

MEN. And did you not think that he knew?

SOC. I have not a good memory, Meno, and therefore I cannot now tell
what I thought of him at the time. And I dare say that he did know,
and that you know what he said: please, therefore, do remind me of
d what he said; or, if you would rather, tell me your own view; for I suspect that you and he think much alike.

MEN. Very true.

SOC. Then as he is not here, never mind him, and do you tell me: By the gods, Meno, be generous and tell me what you say that virtue is; for I shall be truly delighted to find that I have been mistaken, and that you and Gorgias do really have this knowledge, although I have been just saying that I have never found anybody who had.

e *MEN.* There will be no difficulty, Socrates, in answering your question. Let
us take first the virtue of a man—he should know how to administer
the state, and in the administration of it to benefit his friends and
harm his enemies; and he must also be careful not to suffer harm
himself. A woman's virtue, if you wish to know about that, may also be
easily described: her duty is to order her house and keep what is
indoors, and obey her husband. Every age, every condition of life,
young or old, male or female, bond or free, has a different virtue:
72a there are virtues numberless, and no lack of definitions of them; for
virtue is relative to the actions and ages of each of us in all that we do.
And the same may be said of vice, Socrates.[1]

SOC. How fortunate I am, Meno! When I ask you for one virtue, you present me with a swarm of them,[2] which are in your keeping. Suppose
b that I carry on the figure of the swarm, and ask of you, What is the
nature of the bee? And you answer that there are many kinds of bees,
and I reply: But do bees differ as bees because there are many and
different kinds of them; or are they not rather to be distinguished by

some other quality, as, for example, beauty, size, or shape? How
would you answer me?

Men. I should answer that bees do not differ from one another, as bees.

Soc. And if I went on to say: That is what I desire to know, Meno; tell me c
what is the quality in which they do not differ, but are all alike—would
you be able to answer?

Men. I should.

Soc. And so of the virtues, however many and different they may be, they
have all a common nature which makes them virtues; and on this he
who would answer the question, "What is virtue?" would do well to d
have his eye fixed; do you understand?

Men. I am beginning to understand; but I do not as yet take hold of the
question as I could wish.

Soc. When you say, Meno, that there is one virtue of a man, another of a
woman, another of a child, and so on, does this apply only to virtue, or
would you say the same of health, and size, and strength? Or is the e
nature of health always the same, whether in man or woman?

Men. I should say that health is the same, both in man and woman.

Soc. And is not this true of size and strength? If a woman is strong, she will
be strong by reason of the same form and of the same strength subsisting
in her which there is in the man—I mean to say that strength, as strength,
whether of man or woman, is the same. Is there any difference?

Men. I think not.

Soc. And will not virtue, as virtue, be the same, whether in a child or in a 73a
grown-up person, in a woman or in a man?

Men. I cannot help feeling, Socrates, that this case is different from the
others.

Soc. But why? Were you not saying that the virtue of a man was to order a
state, and the virtue of a woman was to order a house?

Men. I did say so.

Soc. And can either house or state or anything be well ordered without
temperance and without justice?

Men. Certainly not.

Soc. Then they who order a state or a house temperately or justly order b
them with temperance and justice?

Men. Certainly.

Soc. Then both men and women, if they are to be good men and women,
must have the same virtues of temperance and justice?

Men. True.

Soc. And can either a young man or an elder one be good if they are intemperate and unjust?

Men. They cannot.

Soc. They must be temperate and just?

c *Men.* Yes.

Soc. Then all men are good in the same way, and by participation in the same virtues?

Men. Such is the inference.

Soc. And they surely would not have been good in the same way unless their virtue had been the same?

Men. They would not.

Soc. Then now that the sameness of all virtue has been proven, try and remember what you and Gorgias say that virtue is.

d *Men.* Will you have one definition of them all?

Soc. That is what I am seeking.

Men. If you want to have one definition of them all, I know not what to say but that virtue is the power of governing mankind.

Soc. And does this definition of virtue include all virtue? Is virtue the same in a child and in a slave, Meno? Can the child govern his father, or the slave his master; and would he who governed be any longer a slave?

Men. I think not, Socrates.

Soc. No, indeed; there would be small reason in that. Yet once more, fair friend; according to you, virtue is "the power of governing"; but do you not add "justly and not unjustly"?

Men. Yes, Socrates; I agree there; for justice is virtue.

e *Soc.* Would you say "virtue," Meno, or "a virtue"?

Men. What do you mean?

Soc. I mean as I might say about anything; that a round, for example, is "a figure" and not simply "figure," and I should adopt this mode of speaking, because there are other figures.

Men. Quite right; and that is just what I am saying about virtue—that there are other virtues as well as justice.

74a *Soc.* What are they? Tell me the names of them, as I would tell you the names of the other figures if you asked me.

Men. Courage and temperance and wisdom and magnanimity are virtues; and there are many others.

Soc. Yes, Meno; and again we are in the same case: in searching after one virtue we have found many, though not in the same way as before; but we have been unable to find the common virtue which runs through them all.

Men. Why, Socrates, even now I am not able to follow you in the attempt b
to get at one common notion of virtue as of other things.

Soc. No wonder; but I will try to get nearer if I can, for you know that all things have a common notion. Suppose now that someone asked you the question which I asked before: Meno, he would say, what is figure? And if you answered "roundness," he would reply to you, in my way of speaking, by asking whether you would say that roundness is "figure" or "a figure"; and you would answer "a figure."

Men. Certainly.

Soc. And for this reason—that there are other figures? c

Men. Yes.

Soc. And if he proceeded to ask, What other figures are there? You would have told him.

Men. I should.

Soc. And if he similarly asked what color is, and you answered whiteness, and the questioner rejoined, Would you say that whiteness is color or a color? You would reply, A color, because there are other colors as well.

Men. I should.

Soc. And if he had said, Tell me what they are? You would have told him d
of other colors which are colors just as much as whiteness.

Men. Yes.

Soc. And suppose that he were to pursue the matter in my way, he would say: Ever and anon we are landed in particulars, but this is not what I want; tell me then, since you call them by a common name and say that they are all figures, even when opposed to one another, what is that common nature which you designate as figure—which contains straight as well as round, and is no more one than the other—that e
would be your mode of speaking?

Men. Yes.

Soc. And in speaking thus, you do not mean to say that the round is round any more than straight, or the straight any more straight than round?

Men. Certainly not.

Soc. You only assert that the round figure is not more a figure than the straight, or the straight than the round?

Men. Very true.

Soc. To what then do we give the name of figure? Try and answer. Suppose
that when a person asked you this question either about figure or 75a

color, you were to reply, Man, I do not understand what you want, or know what you are saying; he would look rather astonished and say: Do you not understand that I am looking for the "*simile in multis*"? And then he might put the question in another form: Meno, he might say, what is that "*simile in multis*" which you call "figure," and which includes not only round and straight figures, but all? Could you not answer that question, Meno? I wish that you would try; the attempt will be good practice with a view to the answer about virtue.

b *Men.* I would rather that you answer, Socrates.

Soc. Shall I indulge you?

Men. By all means.

Soc. And then you will tell me about virtue?

Men. I will.

Soc. Then I must do my best, for there is a prize to be won.

Men. Certainly.

Soc. Well, I will try and explain to you what figure is. What do you say to
this answer? Figure is the only thing which always follows color. Will
c you be satisfied with it, as I am sure that I should be if you would let
me have a similar definition of virtue?

Men. But, Socrates, it is such a simple answer.

Soc. Why simple?

Men. Because, according to you, figure is that which always follows color. (*Soc.* Granted.)

Men. But if a person were to say that he does not know what color is, any more than what figure is—what sort of answer would you have given him?

Soc. I should have told him the truth. And if he were a philosopher of the
d eristic and antagonistic sort, I should say to him: You have my answer,
and if I am wrong, your business is to take up the argument and refute
me. But if we were friends, and were talking as you and I are now, I
should reply in a milder strain and more in the dialectician's vein;
that is to say, I should not only speak the truth, but I should make use
of premises which the person interrogated would be willing to admit.
And this is the way in which I shall endeavor to approach you. You
e will acknowledge, will you not, that there is such a thing as an end, or
termination, or extremity? All which words I use in the same sense,
although I am aware that Prodicus might draw distinctions about them;
but still you, I am sure, would speak of a thing as ended or terminated—
that is all which I am saying—not anything very difficult.

Men. Yes, I should; and I believe that I understand your meaning.

Soc. And you would speak of a surface and also of a solid, as for example 76a
in geometry.

Men. Yes.

Soc. Well then, you are now in a condition to understand my definition of figure. I define figure to be that in which the solid ends; or, more concisely, the limit of solid.

Men. And now, Socrates, what is color?

Soc. You are outrageous, Meno, in thus plaguing a poor old man to give
you an answer, when you will not take the trouble of remembering b
what is Gorgias' definition of virtue.

Men. When you have told me what I ask, I will tell you, Socrates.

Soc. A man who was blindfolded has only to hear you talking, and he would know that you are a fair creature and have still many lovers.

Men. Why do you think so?

Soc. Why, because you always speak in imperatives; like all beauties when they are in their prime, you are tyrannical; and also, as I suspect, you
have found out that I have a weakness for the fair, and therefore to c
humor you I must answer.

Men. Please do.

Soc. Would you like me to answer you after the manner of Gorgias, which is familiar to you?

Men. I should like nothing better.

Soc. Do not he and you and Empedocles say that there are certain effluences of existence?

Men. Certainly.

Soc. And passages into which and through which the effluences pass?

Men. Exactly.

Soc. And some of the effluences fit into the passages, and some of them d
are too small or too large?

Men. True.

Soc. And there is such a thing as sight?

Men. Yes.

Soc. And now, as Pindar says, "read my meaning": color is an effluence of form, commensurate with sight, and palpable to sense.

Men. That, Socrates, appears to me to be an admirable answer.

Soc. Why, yes, because it happens to be one which you have been in the habit of hearing: and your wit will have discovered, I suspect, that you
may explain in the same way the nature of sound and smell, and of e
many other similar phenomena.

Men. Quite true.

Soc. The answer, Meno, was in the orthodox solemn vein, and therefore was more acceptable to you than the other answer about figure.

Men. Yes.

Soc. And yet, O son of Alexidemus, I cannot help thinking that the other was the better; and I am sure that you would be of the same opinion if you would only stay and be initiated, and were not compelled, as you said yesterday, to go away before the mysteries.

77a *Men.* But I will stay, Socrates, if you will give me many such answers.

Soc. Well then, for my own sake as well as for yours, I will do my very best; but I am afraid that I shall not be able to give you very many as good; and now, in your turn, you are to fullfill your promise, and tell me what virtue is in the universal; and do not make a singular into a plural, as the facetious say of those who break a thing, but deliver virtue to me whole and sound, and not broken into a number of pieces; I
b have given you the pattern.

Men. Well then, Socrates, virtue, as I take it, is when he, who desires the honorable, is able to provide it for himself; so the poet says, and I say, too—

Virtue is the desire of things honorable and the power of attaining them.

Soc. And does he who desires the honorable also desire the good?

Men. Certainly.

Soc. Then are there some who desire the evil and others who desire the
c good? Do not all men, my dear sir, desire good?

Men. I think not.

Soc. There are some who desire evil?

Men. Yes.

Soc. Do you mean that they think the evils which they desire to be good; or do they know that they are evil and yet desire them?

Men. Both, I think.

Soc. And do you really imagine, Meno, that a man knows evils to be evils and desires them notwithstanding?

Men. Certainly I do.

Soc. And desire is of possession?

Men. Yes, of possession.

d *Soc.* And does he think that the evils will do good to him who possesses them, or does he know that they will do him harm?

Men. There are some who think that the evils will do them good, and others who know that they will do them harm.

Soc. And, in your opinion, do those who think that they will do them good know that they are evils?

Men. Certainly not.

Soc. Is it not obvious that those who are ignorant of their nature do not desire them; but they desire what they suppose to be goods although
they are really evils; and if they are mistaken and suppose the evils to e
be goods, they really desire goods?

Men. Yes, in that case.

Soc. Well, and do those who, as you say, desire evils, and think that evils are hurtful to the possessor of them, know that they will be hurt by them?

Men. They must know it.

Soc. And must they not suppose that those who are hurt are miserable in 78a
proportion to the hurt which is inflicted upon them?

Men. How can it be otherwise?

Soc. But are not the miserable ill fated?

Men. Yes, indeed.

Soc. And does anyone desire to be miserable and ill fated?

Men. I should say not, Socrates.

Soc. But if there is no one who desires to be miserable, there is no one, Meno, who desires evil; for what is misery but the desire and possession of evil?

Men. That appears to be the truth, Socrates, and I admit that nobody b
desires evil.

Soc. And yet, were you not saying just now that virtue is the desire and power of attaining good?

Men. Yes, I did say so.

Soc. But if this be affirmed, then the desire of good is common to all, and one man is no better than another in that respect?

Men. True.

Soc. And if one man is not better than another in desiring good, he must be better in the power of attaining it?

Men. Exactly.

Soc. Then, according to your definition, virtue would appear to be the c
power of attaining good?

Men. I entirely approve, Socrates, of the manner in which you now view this matter.

Soc. Then let us see whether what you say is true from another point of view; for very likely you may be right—you affirm virtue to be the power of attaining goods?

MEN. Yes.

SOC. And the goods which you mean are such as health and wealth and the possession of gold and silver, and having office and honor in the state—those are what you would call goods?

MEN. Yes, I should include all those.

d *SOC.* Then, according to Meno, who is the hereditary friend of the great king, virtue is the power of getting silver and gold; and would you add that they must be gained piously, justly, or do you deem this to be of no consequence? And is any mode of acquisition, even if unjust and dishonest, equally to be deemed virtue?

MEN. Not virtue, Socrates, but vice.

SOC. Then justice or temperance or holiness, or some other part of virtue, as would appear, must accompany the acquisition, and without them the mere acquisition of good will not be virtue.

MEN. Why, how can there be virtue without these?

SOC. And the non-acquisition of gold and silver in a dishonest manner for
e oneself or another; or, in other words, the want of them may be equally virtue?

MEN. True.

SOC. Then the acquisition of such goods is no more virtue than the non-acquisition and want of them, but whatever is accompanied by justice or honesty is virtue, and whatever is devoid of justice is vice.

MEN. It cannot be otherwise, in my judgment.

79a *SOC.* And were we not saying just now that justice, temperance, and the like, were each of them a part of virtue?

MEN. Yes.

SOC. And so, Meno, this is the way in which you mock me.

MEN. Why do you say that, Socrates?

SOC. Why, because I asked you to deliver virtue into my hands whole and unbroken, and I gave you a pattern according to which you were to
b frame your answer; and you have forgotten already and tell me that virtue is the power of attaining good justly, or with justice; and justice you acknowledge to be a part of virtue.

MEN. Yes.

SOC. Then it follows from your own admissions that virtue is doing what you do with a part of virtue; for justice and the like are said by you to be parts of virtue.

MEN. What of that?

Soc. What of that! Why, did not I ask you to tell me the nature of virtue as
a whole? And you are very far from telling me this, but declare every
action to be virtue which is done with a part of virtue, as though you
had told me and I must already know the whole of virtue, and this, too, c
when frittered away into little pieces. And, therefore, my dear Meno, I
fear that I must begin again and repeat the same question: What is
virtue? For otherwise I can only say that every action done with a part
of virtue is virtue; what else is the meaning of saying that every action
done with justice is virtue? Ought I not to ask the question over again;
for can anyone who does not know virtue know a part of virtue?

Men. No; I do not say that he can.

Soc. Do you remember how, in the example of figure, we rejected any d
answer given in terms which were as yet unexplained or unadmitted?

Men. Yes, Socrates; and we were quite right in doing so.

Soc. But then, my friend, do not suppose that we can explain to anyone
the nature of virtue as a whole through some unexplained portion of
virtue, or anything at all in that fashion; we should only have to ask e
over again the old question, What is virtue? Am I not right?

Men. I believe that you are.

Soc. Then begin again, and answer me. What, according to you and your friend Gorgias, is the definition of virtue?

Men. O Socrates, I used to be told, before I knew you, that you were always
doubting yourself and making others doubt; and now you are casting 80a
your spells over me, and I am simply getting bewitched and enchanted,
and am at my wits' end. And if I may venture to make a jest upon you,
you seem to me both in your appearance and in your power over others
to be very like the flat torpedo fish, who torpifies those who come near
him and touch him, as you have now torpified me, I think. For my b
soul and my tongue are really torpid, and I do not know how to answer
you; and though I have been delivered of an infinite variety of speeches
about virtue before now, and to many persons—and very good ones
they were, as I thought—at this moment I cannot even say what virtue
is. And I think that you are very wise in not voyaging and going away
from home, for if you did in other places as you do in Athens, you
would be cast into prison as a magician.

Soc. You are a rogue, Meno, and had all but caught me.

Men. What do you mean, Socrates?

Soc. I can tell why you made a simile about me. c

Men. Why?

Soc. In order that I might make another simile about you. For I know that all pretty young gentlemen like to have pretty similes made about them—as well they may—but I shall not return the compliment. As to my being a torpedo, if the torpedo is torpid as well as the cause of torpidity in others, then indeed I am a torpedo, but not otherwise; for I perplex others, not because I am clear, but because
d I am utterly perplexed myself. And now I know not what virtue is, and you seem to be in the same case, although you did once perhaps know, before you touched me. However, I have no objection to join with you in the inquiry.

Men. And how will you inquire, Socrates, into that which you do not know? What will you put forth as the subject of inquiry? And if you find what you want, how will you ever know that this is the thing which you did not know?

e *Soc.* I know, Meno, what you mean; but just see what a tiresome dispute you are introducing. You argue that a man cannot inquire either about that which he knows, or about that which he does not know; for if he knows, he has no need to inquire; and if not, he cannot; for he does not know the very subject about which he is to inquire.[3]

81a *Men.* Well, Socrates, and is not the argument sound?

Soc. I think not.

Men. Why not?

Soc. I will tell you why: I have heard from certain wise men and women who spoke of things divine that—

Men. What did they say?

Soc. They spoke of a glorious truth, as I conceive.

Men. What was it and who were they?

Soc. Some of them were priests and priestesses who had studied how they might be able to give a reason of their profession; there have been
b poets also who spoke of these things by inspiration, like Pindar and many others who were inspired. And they say—mark now and see whether their words are true—they say that the soul of man is immortal, and at one time has an end, which is termed dying, and at another time is born again, but is never destroyed. And the moral is that a man ought to live always in perfect holiness. "For in the ninth year Persephone sends the souls of those from whom she has received the penalty of ancient crime back again from beneath into the light of
c the sun above, and these are they who become noble kings and mighty

men and great in wisdom and are called saintly heroes in after-ages."
The soul, then, as being immortal, and having been born again many d
times, and having seen all things that exist, whether in this world or in the world below, has knowledge of them all; and it is no wonder that she should be able to call to remembrance all that she ever knew about virtue and about everything; for as all nature is akin, and the soul has learned all things, there is no difficulty in her eliciting, or as men say "learning," out of a single recollection, all the rest, if a man is strenuous and does not faint; for all inquiry and all learning is but recollection. And therefore we ought not to listen to this sophistical argument about the impossibility of inquiry; for it will make us idle,
and is sweet only to the sluggard; but the other saying will make us e
active and inquisitive. In that confiding, I will gladly inquire with you into the nature of virtue.

MEN. Yes, Socrates; but what do you mean by saying that we do not learn, and that what we call learning is only a process of recollection? Can you teach me how this is?

SOC. I told you, Meno, just now that you were a rogue, and now you ask
whether I can teach you, when I am saying that there is no teaching, 82a
but only recollection; and thus you imagine that you will involve me in a contradiction.

MEN. Indeed, Socrates, I protest that I had no such intention. I only asked the question from habit; but if you can prove to me that what you say is true, I wish that you would.

SOC. It will be no easy matter, but I will try to please you to the utmost of
my power. Suppose that you call one of your numerous attendants, b
that I may demonstrate on him.

MEN. Certainly. Come hither, boy.

SOC. He is Greek, and speaks Greek, does he not?

MEN. Yes, indeed; he was born in the house.

SOC. Attend now to the questions which I ask him, and observe whether he learns of me or only remembers.

MEN. I will.

SOC. Tell me, boy, do you know that a figure like this is a square?[*]

BOY. I do.

SOC. And you know that a square figure has these four lines equal? c

BOY. Certainly.

SOC. And these lines which I have drawn through the middle of the square are also equal?[‡]

Boy. Yes.

Soc. A square may be of any size?

Boy. Certainly.

Soc. And if one side of the figure be of two feet, and the other side be of two feet, how much will the whole be? Let me explain: if in one direction the space was of two feet, and in the other direction of one foot, the whole would be of two feet taken once?

Boy. Yes.

Soc. But since this side is also of two feet, there are twice two feet?

Boy. There are.

Soc. Then the square is of twice two feet?

Boy. Yes.

d *Soc.* And how many are twice two feet? Count and tell me.

Boy. Four, Socrates.

Soc. And might there not be another square twice as large as this, and having like this the lines equal?

Boy. Yes.

Soc. And of how many feet will that be?

Boy. Of eight feet.

Soc. And now try and tell the length of the line which forms the side of
e that double square: this is two feet—what will that be?

Boy. Clearly, Socrates, it will be double.

Soc. Do you observe, Meno, that I am not teaching the boy anything, but only asking him questions; and now he fancies that he knows how long a line is necessary in order to produce a figure of eight square feet; does he not?

Men. Yes.

Soc. And does he really know?

Men. Certainly not.

Soc. He only guesses that because the square is double, the line is double.

Men. True.

Soc. Observe him while he recalls the steps in regular order. (*To the Boy.*) Tell me, boy, do you assert that a double space comes from a double
83a line? Remember[†] that I am not speaking of an oblong, but of a figure equal every way, and twice the size of this—that is to say of eight feet; and I want to know whether you still say that a double square comes from a double line?

Boy. Yes.

Soc. But does not this line become doubled if we add another such line here?

Boy. Certainly. b

Soc. And four such lines will make a space containing eight feet?

Boy. Yes.

Soc. Let us describe such a figure: Would you not say that this is the figure of eight feet?

Boy. Yes.

Soc. And are there not these four divisions in the figure, each of which is equal to the figure of four feet?

Boy. True.

Soc. And is not that four times four?

Boy. Certainly.

Soc. And four times is not double?

Boy. No, indeed.

Soc. But how much?

Boy. Four times as much.

Soc. Therefore the double line, boy, has given a space, not twice, but four c
times as much.

Boy. True.

Soc. Four times four are sixteen—are they not?

Boy. Yes.

Soc. What line would give you a space of eight feet, as this gives one of sixteen feet—do you see?

Boy. Yes.

Soc. And the space of four feet is made from this half line?

Boy. Yes.

Soc. Good; and is not a space of eight feet twice the size of this, and half the size of the other?

Boy. Certainly.

Soc. Such a space, then, will be made out of a line greater than this one, and less than that one?

Boy. Yes, I think so. d

Soc. Very good; I like to hear you say what you think. And now tell me, is not this a line of two feet and that of four?

Boy. Yes.

Soc. Then the line which forms the side of eight feet ought to be more than this line of two feet, and less than the other of four feet?

Boy. It ought.

e *Soc.* Try and see if you can tell me how much it will be.

Boy. Three feet.[Φ]

Soc. Then if we add a half to this line of two, that will be the line of three. Here are two and there is one; and on the other side, here are two also and there is one: and that makes the figure of which you speak?

Boy. Yes.

Soc. But if there are three feet this way and three feet that way, the whole space will be three times three feet?

Boy. That is evident.

Soc. And how much are three times three feet?

Boy. Nine.

Soc. And how much is the double of four?

Boy. Eight.

Soc. Then the figure of eight is not made out of a line of three?

Boy. No.

84a *Soc.* But from what line? Tell me exactly; and if you would rather not reckon, try and show me the line.

Boy. Indeed, Socrates, I do not know.

Soc. Do you see, Meno, what advances he has made in his power of recollection? He did not know at first, and he does not know now, what is the side of a figure of eight feet; but then he thought that he knew, and answered confidently as if he knew, and had no difficulty; now he
b has a difficulty, and neither knows nor fancies that he knows.

Men. True.

Soc. Is he not better off in knowing his ignorance?

Men. I think that he is.

Soc. If we have made him doubt, and given him the "torpedo's shock," have we done him any harm?

Men. I think not.

Soc. We have certainly, as would seem, assisted him in some degree to the
c discovery of the truth; and now he will wish to remedy his ignorance, but then he would have been ready to tell all the world again and again that the double space should have a double side.

Men. True.

Soc. But do you suppose that he would ever have inquired into or learned what he fancied that he knew, though he was really ignorant of it, until he had fallen into perplexity under the idea that he did not know, and had desired to know?

Men. I think not, Socrates.

Soc. Then he was the better for the torpedo's touch?

Men. I think so.

Soc. Mark now the further development. I shall only ask him, and not
teach him, and he shall share the inquiry with me; and do you watch d
and see if you find me telling or explaining anything to him, instead of eliciting his opinion. Tell me, boy, is not this a square of four feet which I have drawn?

Boy. Yes.

Soc. And now I add another square equal to the former one?

Boy. Yes.

Soc. And a third, which is equal to either of them?

Boy. Yes.

Soc. Suppose that we fill up the vacant corner?

Boy. Very good.

Soc. Here, then, there are four equal spaces?

Boy. Yes. e

Soc. And how many times larger is this space than this other?

Boy. Four times.

Soc. But it ought to have been twice only, as you will remember.

Boy. True.

Soc. And does not this line, reaching from corner to corner, bisect each 85a
of these spaces?[Ψ]

Boy. Yes.

Soc. And are there not here four equal lines which contain this space?

Boy. There are.

Soc. Look and see how much this space is.

Boy. I do not understand.

Soc. Has not each interior line cut off half of the four spaces?

Boy. Yes.

Soc. And how many spaces are there in this section?

Boy. Four.

Sac. And how many in this?

Boy. Two.

Soc. And four is how many times two?

Boy. Twice.

Soc. And this space is of how many feet?

Boy. Of eight feet. b

Soc. And from what line do you get this figure?

Boy. From this.

Soc. That is, from the line which extends from corner to corner of the figure of four feet?

Boy. Yes.

Soc. And this is the line which the learned call the diagonal. And if this is the proper name, then you, Meno's slave, are prepared to affirm that the double space is the square of the diagonal?

Boy. Certainly, Socrates.

Soc. What do you say of him, Meno? Were not all these answers given out of his own head?

c *Men.* Yes, they were all his own.

Soc. And yet, as we were just now saying, he did not know?

Men. True.

Soc. But still he had in him those notions of his—had he not?

Men. Yes.

Soc. Then he who does not know may still have true notions of that which he does not know?

Men. He has.

Soc. And at present these notions have just been stirred up in him, as in a dream; but if he were frequently asked the same questions, in different
d forms, he would know as well as anyone at last?

Men. I dare say.

Soc. Without anyone teaching him he will recover his knowledge for himself, if he is only asked questions?

Men. Yes.

Soc. And this spontaneous recovery of knowledge in him is recollection?

Men. True.

Soc. And this knowledge which he now has must he not either have acquired or always possessed?

Men. Yes.

Soc. But if he always possessed this knowledge he would always have known; or if he has acquired the knowledge he could not have acquired it in this life unless he has been taught geometry; for he may be made
e to do the same with all geometry and every other branch of knowledge. Now, has anyone ever taught him all this? You must know about him if, as you say, he was born and bred in your house.

Men. And I am certain that no one ever did teach him.

Soc. And yet he has the knowledge?

Men. The fact, Socrates, is undeniable.

Soc. But if he did not acquire the knowledge in this life, then he must have 86a
had and learned it at some other time?

Men. Clearly he must.

Soc. Which must have been the time when he was not a man?

Men. Yes.

Soc. And if there have been always true thoughts in him, both at the time when he was and was not a man, which only need to be awakened into knowledge by putting questions to him, his soul must have always possessed this knowledge, for he always either was or was not a man?

Men. Obviously.

Soc. And if the truth of all things always existed in the soul, then the soul b
is immortal. Wherefore be of good cheer and try to recollect what you
do not know, or rather what you do not remember.

Men. I feel, somehow, that I like what you are saying.

Soc. And I, Meno, like what I am saying. Some things I have said of which
I am not altogether confident. But that we shall be better and braver
and less helpless if we think that we ought to inquire than we should
have been if we indulged in the idle fancy that there was no knowing
and no use in seeking to know what we do not know—that is a theme c
upon which I am ready to fight, in word and deed, to the utmost of
my power.

Men. There again, Socrates, your words seem to me excellent.

Soc. Then, as we are agreed that a man should inquire about that which he does not know, shall you and I make an effort to inquire together into the nature of virtue?

Men. By all means, Socrates. And yet I would much rather return to my
original question, Whether in seeking to acquire virtue we should
regard it as a thing to be taught, or as a gift of nature, or as coming to d
men in some other way?

Soc. Had I the command of you as well as of myself, Meno, I would not
have inquired whether virtue is given by instruction or not, until we
had first ascertained "what it is." But as you think only of controlling e
me who am your slave, and never of controlling yourself—such being
your notion of freedom—I must yield to you, for you are irresistible.
And therefore I have now to inquire into the qualities of a thing of
which I do not as yet know the nature. At any rate, will you condescend a little and allow the question "Whether virtue is given by
instruction, or in any other way," to be argued upon hypothesis? As
the geometrician, when he is asked whether a certain triangle is

87a capable of being inscribed in a certain circle,[4] will reply: "I cannot tell you as yet, but I will offer a hypothesis which may assist us in forming a conclusion. If the figure be such that when you have produced a given side of it,[5] the given area of the triangle falls short by an area corresponding to the part produced,[6] then one consequence follows, and if this is impossible, then some other; and therefore I
b wish to assume a hypothesis before I tell you whether this triangle is capable of being inscribed in the circle"—that is a geometrical hypothesis. And we too, as we know not the nature and qualities of virtue, must ask whether virtue is or is not taught, under a hypothesis:
c as thus, if virtue is of such a class of mental goods, will it be taught or not? Let the first hypothesis be that virtue is or is not knowledge—in that case will it be taught or not, or, as we were just now saying, "remembered"? For there is no use in disputing about the name. But is virtue taught or not, or rather, does not everyone see that knowledge alone is taught?

MEN. I agree.

SOC. Then if virtue is knowledge, virtue will be taught?

MEN. Certainly.

SOC. Then now we have made a quick end of this question: if virtue is of such a nature, it will be taught; and if not, not?

MEN. Certainly.

SOC. The next question is whether virtue is knowledge or of another species?

d *MEN.* Yes, that appears to be the question which comes next in order.

SOC. Do we not say that virtue is a good? This is a hypothesis which is not set aside.

MEN. Certainly.

SOC. Now, if there be any sort of good which is distinct from knowledge, virtue may be that good; but if knowledge embraces all good, then we shall be right in thinking that virtue is knowledge?

MEN. True.

SOC. And virtue makes us good?

e *MEN.* Yes.

SOC. And if we are good, then we are profitable; for all good things are profitable?

MEN. Yes.

SOC. Then virtue is profitable?

MEN. That is the only inference.

Soc. Then now let us see what are the things which severally profit us. Health and strength, and beauty and wealth—these, and the like of these, we call profitable?

Men. True. 88a

Soc. And yet these things may also sometimes do us harm, would you not think so?

Men. Yes.

Soc. And what is the guiding principle which makes them profitable or the reverse? Are they not profitable when they are rightly used, and harmful when they are not rightly used?

Men. Certainly.

Soc. Next, let us consider the goods of the soul: they are temperance, justice, courage, quickness of apprehension, memory, magnanimity, and the like?

Men. Surely. b

Soc. And such of these as are not knowledge, but of another sort, are sometimes profitable and sometimes hurtful; as, for example, courage wanting prudence, which is only a sort of confidence? When a man has no sense he is harmed by courage, but when he has sense he is profited?

Men. True.

Soc. And the same may be said of temperance and quickness of apprehension; whatever things are learned or done with sense are profitable, but when done without sense they are hurtful?

Men. Very true.

Soc. And in general, all that the soul attempts or endures, when under c
the guidance of wisdom, ends in happiness; but when she is under the
guidance of folly, in the opposite?

Men. That appears to be true.

Soc. If then virtue is a quality of the soul, and is admitted to be profitable, it must be wisdom or prudence, since none of the things of the
soul are either profitable or hurtful in themselves, but they are all
made profitable or hurtful by the addition of wisdom or of folly;
and therefore, if virtue is profitable, virtue must be a sort of wisdom d
or prudence?

Men. I quite agree.

Soc. And the other goods, such as wealth and the like, of which we were just now saying that they are sometimes good and sometimes evil, do not they also become profitable or hurtful, accordingly as the soul e guides and uses them rightly or wrongly; just as the things of the soul herself are benefited when under the guidance of wisdom, and harmed by folly?

MEN. True.

SOC. And the wise soul guides them rightly, and the foolish soul wrongly?

MEN. Yes.

SOC. And is not this universally true of human nature? All other things hang upon the soul, and the things of the soul herself hang upon
89a wisdom, if they are to be good; and so wisdom is inferred to be that which profits—and virtue, as we say, is profitable?

MEN. Certainly.

SOC. And thus we arrive at the conclusion that virtue is either wholly or partly wisdom?

MEN. I think that what you are saying, Socrates, is very true.

SOC. But if this is true, then the good are not by nature good?

MEN. I think not.

b *SOC.* If they had been, there would assuredly have been discerners of characters among us who would have known our future great men; and on their showing we should have adopted them, and when we had got them, we should have kept them in the citadel out of the way of harm, and set a stamp upon them far rather than upon a piece of gold, in order that no one might tamper with them; and when they grew up they would have been useful to the state?

MEN. Yes, Socrates, that would have been the right way.

c *SOC.* But if the good are not by nature good, are they made good by instruction?

MEN. There appears to be no other alternative, Socrates. On the supposition that virtue is knowledge, there can be no doubt that virtue is taught.

SOC. Yes, indeed; but what if the supposition is erroneous?

MEN. I certainly thought just now that we were right.

SOC. Yes, Meno; but a principle which has any soundness should stand firm not only just now, but always.

d *MEN.* Well; and why are you so slow of heart to believe that knowledge is virtue?

SOC. I will try and tell you why, Meno. I do not retract the assertion that if virtue is knowledge it may be taught; but I fear that I have some reason in doubting whether virtue is knowledge; for consider now and say whether virtue, and not only virtue but anything that is taught, must not have teachers and disciples?

Men. Surely.

Soc. And conversely, may not the art of which neither teachers nor disci- e
ples exist be assumed to be incapable of being taught?

Men. True; but do you think that there are no teachers of virtue?

Soc. I have certainly often inquired whether there were any, and taken
great pains to find them, and have never succeeded; and many have
assisted me in the search, and they were the persons whom I thought
the most likely to know. Here at the moment when he is wanted
we fortunately have sitting by us Anytus, the very person of whom we 90a
should make inquiry; to him then let us repair. In the first place, he is
the son of a wealthy and wise father, Anthemion, who acquired his
wealth, not by accident or gift, like Ismenias the Theban (who has
recently made himself as rich as Polycrates), but by his own skill and
industry, and who is a well-conditioned, modest man, not insolent, or
overbearing, or annoying; moreover, this son of his has received a good
education, as the Athenian people certainly appear to think, for they b
choose him to fill the highest offices. And these are the sort of men
from whom you are likely to learn whether there are any teachers of
virtue, and who they are. Please, Anytus, to help me and your friend
Meno in answering our question, Who are the teachers? Consider
the matter thus: If we wanted Meno to be a good physician, to whom
should we send him? Should we not send him to the physicians? c

Anytus. Certainly.

Soc. Or if we wanted him to be a good cobbler, should we not send him to the cobblers?

Any. Yes.

Soc. And so forth?

Any. Yes.

Soc. Let me trouble you with one more question. When we say that we
should be right in sending him to the physicians if we wanted him to
be a physician, do we mean that we should be right in sending him d
to those who profess the art rather than to those who do not, and to
those who demand payment for teaching the art and profess to teach
it to anyone who will come and learn? And if these were our reasons,
should we not be right in sending him?

Any. Yes.

Soc. And might not the same be said of flute-playing and of the other arts?
Would a man who wanted to make another a flute-player refuse to e
send him to those who profess to teach the art for money, and be

plaguing other persons to give him instruction, who are not professed teachers and who never had a single disciple in that branch of knowledge which he wishes him to acquire—would not such conduct be the height of folly?

Any. Yes, by Zeus, and of ignorance, too.

Soc. Very good. And now you are in a position to advise with me about my
91a friend Meno. He has been telling me, Anytus, that he desires to attain
that kind of wisdom and virtue by which men order the state or the
house, and honor their parents, and know when to receive and when to
b send away citizens and strangers, as a good man should. Now, to whom
should he go in order that he may learn this virtue? Does not the previous argument imply clearly that we should send him to those who profess and avouch that they are the common teachers of all Hellas, and are ready to impart instruction to anyone who likes, at a fixed price?

Any. Whom do you mean, Socrates?

Soc. You surely know, do you not, Anytus, that these are the people whom mankind call Sophists?

c *Any.* By Heracles, Socrates, forebear! I only hope that no friend or kinsman or acquaintance of mine, whether citizen or stranger, will ever be so mad as to allow himself to be corrupted by them; for they are a manifest pest and corrupting influence to those who have to do with them.

Soc. What, Anytus? Of all the people who profess that they know how to
do men good, do you mean to say that these are the only ones who not
d only do them no good, but positively corrupt those who are entrusted
to them, and in return for this disservice have the face to demand money? Indeed, I cannot believe you; for I know of a single man, Protagoras, who made more out of his craft than the illustrious Phidias, who created such noble works, or any ten other statuaries. How could that be? A mender of old shoes, or patcher-up of clothes, who made
the shoes or clothes worse than he received them, could not have
e remained thirty days undetected, and would very soon have starved;
whereas, during more than forty years, Protagoras was corrupting all Hellas and sending his disciples from him worse than he received them, and he was never found out. For, if I am not mistaken, he was about seventy years old at his death, forty of which were spent in the
practice of his profession; and during all that time he had a good
92a reputation, which to this day he retains: and not only Protagoras, but
many others are well spoken of; some who lived before him, and others who are still living. Now, when you say that they deceived and

corrupted the youth, are they to be supposed to have corrupted them consciously or unconsciously? Can those who were deemed by many to be the wisest men of Hellas have been out of their minds?

Any. Out of their minds! No, Socrates, the young men who gave their
money to them were out of their minds; and their relations and guardians who entrusted their youth to the care of these men were still more b
out of their minds, and most of all, the cities who allowed them to
come in, and did not drive them out, citizen and stranger alike.

Soc. Has any of the Sophists wronged you, Anytus? What makes you so angry with them?

Any. No, indeed, neither I nor any of my belongings has ever had, nor would I suffer them to have, anything to do with them.

Soc. Then you are entirely unacquainted with them?

Any. And I have no wish to be acquainted.

Soc. Then, my dear friend, how can you know whether a thing is good or c
bad of which you are wholly ignorant?

Any. Quite well; I am sure that I know what manner of men these are, whether I am acquainted with them or not.

Soc. You must be a diviner, Anytus, for I really cannot make out, judging
from your own words, how, if you are not acquainted with them, you
know about them. But I am not inquiring of you who are the teachers d
who will corrupt Meno (let them be, if you please, the Sophists); I only
ask you to tell him who there is in this great city who will teach him
how to become eminent in the virtues which I was just now describing.
He is the friend of your family, and you will oblige him.

Any. Why do you not tell him yourself?

Soc. I have told him whom I supposed to be the teachers of these things;
but I learn from you that I am utterly at fault, and I dare say that you
are right. And now I wish that you, on your part, would tell me to e
whom among the Athenians he should go. Whom would you name?

Any. Why single out individuals? Any Athenian gentleman, taken at random, if he will mind him, will do far more good to him than the Sophists.

Soc. And did those gentlemen grow of themselves; and without having
been taught by anyone, were they nevertheless able to teach others
that which they had never learned themselves? 93a

Any. I imagine that they learned of the previous generation of gentlemen. Have there not been many good men in this city?

Soc. Yes, certainly, Anytus; and many good statesmen also there always have been, and there are still, in the city of Athens. But the question is

whether they were also good teachers of their own virtue—not whether
there are, or have been, good men in this part of the world,
but whether virtue can be taught, is the question which we have been
b discussing. Now, do we mean to say that the good men of our own and
of other times knew how to impart to others that virtue which they had
themselves; or is virtue a thing incapable of being communicated or
imparted by one man to another? That is the question which I and
Meno have been arguing. Look at the matter in your own way: Would
c you not admit that Themistocles was a good man?

Any. Certainly; no man better.

Soc. And must not he then have been a good teacher, if any man ever was a good teacher, of his own virtue?

Any. Yes, certainly—if he wanted to be so.

Soc. But would he not have wanted? He would, at any rate, have desired
to make his own son a good man and a gentleman; he could not have
been jealous of him, or have intentionally abstained from imparting to
d him his own virtue. Did you never hear that he made his son Cleophantus a famous horseman; and had him taught to stand upright on
horseback and hurl a javelin, and to do many other marvelous things;
and in anything which could be learned from a master he was well
trained? Have you not heard from our elders of him?

Any. I have.

Soc. Then no one could say that his son showed any want of capacity?

e *Any.* Very likely not.

Soc. But did anyone, old or young, ever say in your hearing that Cleophantus, son of Themistocles, was a wise or good man, as his father was?

Any. I have certainly never heard anyone say so.

Soc. And if virtue could have been taught, would his father Themistocles have sought to train him in these minor accomplishments, and allowed him who, as you must remember, was his own son, to be no better than his neighbors in those qualities in which he himself excelled?

Any. Indeed, indeed, I think not.

Soc. Here was a teacher of virtue whom you admit to be among the best
94a men of the past. Let us take another—Aristides, the son of Lysimachus; would you not acknowledge that he was a good man?

Any. To be sure I should.

Soc. And did not he train his son Lysimachus better than any other Athenian in all that could be done for him by the help of masters? But what has been the result? Is he a bit better than any other mortal? He is an

acquaintance of yours, and you see what he is like. There is Pericles, b
again, magnificent in his wisdom; and he, as you are aware, had two
sons, Paralus and Xanthippus.

Any. I know.

Soc. And you know, also, that he taught them to be unrivaled horsemen,
and had them trained in music and gymnastics and all sorts of arts—in
these respects they were on a level with the best—and had he no wish
to make good men of them? Nay, he must have wished it. But virtue,
as I suspect, could not be taught. And that you may not suppose the
incompetent teachers to be only the meaner sort of Athenians and few
in number, remember again that Thucydides had two sons, Melesias c
and Stephanus, whom, besides giving them a good education in other
things, he trained in wrestling, and they were the best wrestlers in
Athens: one of them he committed to the care of Xanthias, and the
other to Eudorus, who had the reputation of being the most celebrated
wrestlers of that day. Do you remember them?

Any. I have heard of them.

Soc. Now, can there be a doubt that Thucydides, whose children were
taught things for which he had to spend money, would have taught d
them to be good men, which would have cost him nothing, if virtue
could have been taught? Will you reply that he was a mean man, and
had not many friends among the Athenians and allies? Nay, but he
was of a great family, and a man of influence at Athens and in all
Hellas, and, if virtue could have been taught, he would have found
out some Athenian or foreigner who would have made good men of
his sons if he could not himself spare the time from cares of state.
Once more, I suspect, friend Anytus, that virtue is not a thing which e
can be taught.

Any. Socrates, I think that you are too ready to speak evil of men: and, if
you will take my advice, I would recommend you to be careful. Perhaps there is no city in which it is not easier to do men harm than to
do them good, and this is certainly the case at Athens, as I believe 95a
that you know.

Soc. O Meno, I think that Anytus is in a rage. And he may well be in a rage,
for he thinks, in the first place, that I am defaming these gentlemen;
and in the second place, he is of opinion that he is one of them himself. But some day he will know what is the meaning of defamation,
and if he ever does, he will forgive me. Meanwhile I will return to you,
Meno; for I suppose that there are gentlemen in your region, too?

MEN. Certainly there are.

b *SOC.* And are they willing to teach the young, and do they profess to be teachers, and do they agree that virtue is taught?

MEN. No, indeed, Socrates, they are anything but agreed; you may hear them saying at one time that virtue can be taught, and then again the reverse.

SOC. Can we call those "teachers" who do not acknowledge the possibility of their own vocation?

MEN. I think not, Socrates.

SOC. And what do you think of these Sophists, who are the only professors? Do they seem to you to be teachers of virtue?

c *MEN.* I often wonder, Socrates, that Gorgias is never heard promising to teach virtue; and when he hears others promising he only laughs at them, but he thinks that men should be taught to speak.

SOC. Then do you not think that the Sophists are teachers?

MEN. I cannot tell you, Socrates; like the rest of the world, I am in doubt, and sometimes I think that they are teachers, and sometimes not.

SOC. And are you aware that not you only and other politicians have
d doubts whether virtue can be taught or not, but that Theognis the poet says the very same thing?

MEN. Where does he say so?

SOC. In these elegiac verses:

> Eat and drink and sit with the mighty, and make yourself agreeable to them; for from the good you will learn what is good, but if you mix with the bad, you will lose the intelligence which you
> e already have.[7]

Do you observe that here he seems to imply that virtue can be taught?

MEN. Clearly.

SOC. But in some other verses he shifts about and says:[8]

> If understanding could be created and put into a man, then they [who were able to perform this feat] would have obtained great rewards.

And again:

> Never would a bad son have sprung from a good sire, for he would
> 96a have heard the voice of instruction; but not by teaching will you ever make a bad man into a good one.

And this, as you may remark, is a contradiction of the other.

Men. Clearly.

Soc. And is there anything else of which the professors are affirmed not only not to be teachers of others, but to be ignorant themselves, and bad at the knowledge of that which they are professing to teach; or is b
there anything about which even the acknowledged "gentlemen" are sometimes saying that "this thing can be taught," and sometimes the opposite? Can you say that they are teachers in any true sense whose ideas are in such confusion?

Men. I should say, certainly not.

Soc. But if neither the Sophists nor the gentlemen are teachers, clearly there can be no other teachers?

Men. No.

Soc. And if there are no teachers, neither are there disciples? c

Men. Agreed.

Soc. And we have admitted that a thing cannot be taught of which there are neither teachers nor disciples?

Men. We have.

Soc. And there are no teachers of virtue to be found anywhere?

Men. There are not.

Soc. And if there are no teachers, neither are there scholars?

Men. That, I think, is true.

Soc. Then virtue cannot be taught?

Men. Not if we are right in our view. But I cannot believe, Socrates, that there d
are no good men; and if there are, how did they come into existence?

Soc. I am afraid, Meno, that you and I are not good for much, and that Gorgias has been as poor an educator of you as Prodicus has been of me. Certainly we shall have to look to ourselves, and try to find someone who will help in some way of other to improve us. This I say, e
because I observe that in the previous discussion none of us remarked that right and good action is possible to man under other guidance than that of knowledge (*ἐπιστήμη*)—and indeed if this be denied, there is no seeing how there can be any good men at all.

Men. How do you mean, Socrates?

Soc. I mean that good men are necessarily useful or profitable. Were we 97a
not right in admitting this? It must be so.

Men. Yes.

Soc. And in supposing that they will be useful only if they are true guides to us of action—there we were also right?

Men. Yes.

Soc. But when we said that a man cannot be a good guide unless he has knowledge (*φρόνησις*), in this we were wrong.

Men. What do you mean by the word "right"?

Soc. I will explain. If a man knew the way to Larisa, or anywhere else, and went to the place and led others thither, would he not be a right and good guide?

Men. Certainly.

b *Soc.* And a person who had a right opinion about the way, but had never been and did not know, might be a good guide also, might he not?

Men. Certainly.

Soc. And while he has true opinion about that which the other knows, he will be just as good a guide if he thinks the truth, as he who knows the truth?

Men. Exactly.

Soc. Then true opinion is as good a guide to correct action as knowledge;
and that was the point which we omitted in our speculation about the
c nature of virtue, when we said that knowledge only is the guide of right
action; whereas there is also right opinion.

Men. True.

Soc. Then right opinion is not less useful than knowledge?

Men. The difference, Socrates, is only that he who has knowledge will always be right; but he who has right opinion will sometimes be right, and sometimes not.

Soc. What do you mean? Can he be wrong who has right opinion, so long as he has right opinion?

Men. I admit the cogency of your argument, and therefore, Socrates, I
d wonder that knowledge should be preferred to right opinion—or why
they should ever differ.

Soc. And shall I explain this wonder to you?

Men. Do tell me.

Soc. You would not wonder if you had ever observed the images of Daedalus;[9] but perhaps you have not got them in your country?

Men. What have they to do with the question?

Soc. Because they require to be fastened in order to keep them, and if they are not fastened, they will play truant and run away.

e *Men.* Well, what of that?

Soc. I mean to say that they are not very valuable possessions if they are at liberty, for they will walk off like runaway slaves; but when fastened,

they are of great value, for they are really beautiful works of art. Now
this is an illustration of the nature of true opinions: while they abide
with us they are beautiful and fruitful, but they run away out of the
human soul, and do not remain long, and therefore they are not of 98a
much value until they are fastened by the tie of the cause; and this
fastening of them, friend Meno, is recollection, as you and I have
agreed to call it. But when they are bound, in the first place, they
have the nature of knowledge; and, in the second place, they are abiding. And this is why knowledge is more honorable and excellent than true opinion, because fastened by a chain.

Men. What you are saying, Socrates, seems to be very like the truth.

Soc. I, too, speak rather in ignorance; I only conjecture. And yet that b
knowledge differs from true opinion is no matter of conjecture with me. There are not many things which I profess to know, but this is most certainly one of them.

Men. Yes, Socrates; and you are quite right in saying so.

Soc. And am I not also right in saying that true opinion leading the way perfects action quite as well as knowledge?

Men. There again, Socrates, I think you are right.

Soc. Then right opinion is not a whit inferior to knowledge, or less useful c
in action; nor is the man who has right opinion inferior to him who has knowledge?

Men. True.

Soc. And surely the good man has been acknowledged by us to be useful?

Men. Yes.

Soc. Seeing then that men become good and useful to states, not only
because they have knowledge, but because they have right opinion,
and that neither knowledge nor right opinion is given to man by d
nature or acquired by him—(do you imagine either of them to be given by nature?

Men. Not I.)

Soc. Then if they are not given by nature, neither are the good by nature good?

Men. Certainly not.

Soc. And nature being excluded, then came the question whether virtue is acquired by teaching?

Men. Yes.

Soc. If virtue was wisdom [or knowledge], then, as we thought, it was taught?

Men. Yes.

Soc. And if it was taught, it was wisdom?

Men. Certainly.

e *Soc.* And if there were teachers, it might be taught; and if there were no teachers, not?

Men. True.

Soc. But surely we acknowledged that there were no teachers of virtue?

Men. Yes.

Soc. Then we acknowledged that it was not taught, and was not wisdom.

Men. Certainly.

Soc. And yet we admitted that it was a good?

Men. Yes.

Soc. And the right guide is useful and good?

Men. Certainly.

99a *Soc.* And the only right guides are knowledge and true opinion—these are the guides of man; for things which happen by chance are not under the guidance of man; but the guides of man are true opinion and knowledge.

Men. I think so, too.

Soc. But if virtue is not taught, neither is virtue knowledge.

Men. Clearly not.

b *Soc.* Then of two good and useful things, one, which is knowledge, has been set aside and cannot be supposed to be our guide in political life.

Men. I think not.

Soc. And therefore not by any wisdom, and not because they were wise, did Themistocles and those others of whom Anytus spoke govern states. This was the reason why they were unable to make others like themselves—because their virtue was not grounded on knowledge.

Men. That is probably true, Socrates.

Soc. But if not by knowledge, the only alternative which remains is that
c statesmen must have guided states by right opinion, which is in politics what divination is in religion; for diviners and also prophets say many things truly, but they know not what they say.

Men. So I believe.

Soc. And may we not, Meno, truly call those men "divine" who, having no understanding, yet succeed in many a grand deed and word?

Men. Certainly.

Soc. Then we shall also be right in calling divine those whom we were just now speaking of as diviners and prophets, including the whole tribe
d of poets. Yes, and statesmen above all may be said to be divine and

illumined, being inspired and possessed of the god, in which condition they say many grand things, not knowing what they say.

Men. Yes.

Soc. And the women, too, Meno, call good men divine—do they not? And the Spartans, when they praise a good man, say "that he is a divine man."

Men. And I think, Socrates, that they are right, although very likely our e
friend Anytus may take offense at the word.

Soc. I do not care; as for Anytus, there will be another opportunity of talking with him. To sum up our inquiry—the result seems to be, if we are at all right in our view, that virtue is neither natural nor acquired, but
an instinct given by God to the virtuous. Nor is the instinct accompa- 100a
nied by reason, unless there may be supposed to be among statesmen someone who is capable of educating statesmen. And if there be such a one, he may be said to be among the living what Homer says that Tiresias was among the dead, "he alone has understanding; but the rest are flitting shades"; and he and his virtue in like manner will be a reality among shadows.

Men. That is excellent, Socrates. b

Soc. Then, Meno, the conclusion is that virtue comes to the virtuous by divine dispensation. But we shall never know the certain truth until, before asking how virtue is given, we inquire into the actual nature of virtue. I fear that I must go away, but do you, now that you are persuaded yourself, persuade our friend Anytus. And do not let him be so
exasperated; if you can conciliate him, you will have done good service c
to the Athenian people.

Appendix to Meno

by Amit Hagar

* (p. 15) In this famous section of the dialogue, Socrates demonstrates his idea that mathematical (geometrical) knowledge is innate, by teaching a slave boy to double the size of a given square.

Socrates first draws a simple 2f by 2f square ABCD:

‡ (p. 15) He then dissects the square into four:

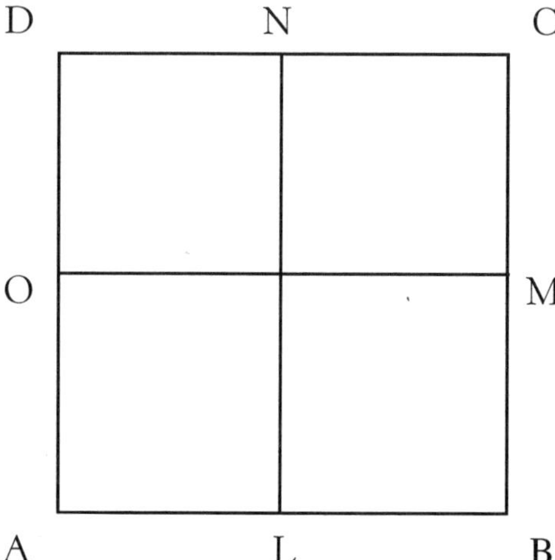

† (p. 16) Using this diagram he probes the slave's understanding of the concept of an *area* of a square. The goal is now to find a line segment (it will be the diagonal) from which one can create a square with an area twice as big as the original square ABCD.

Socrates proceeds by way of elimination. The first, natural, step is to try to double the line DC. This, of course, will yield a square DEFG with an area 4 times as big as ABCD:

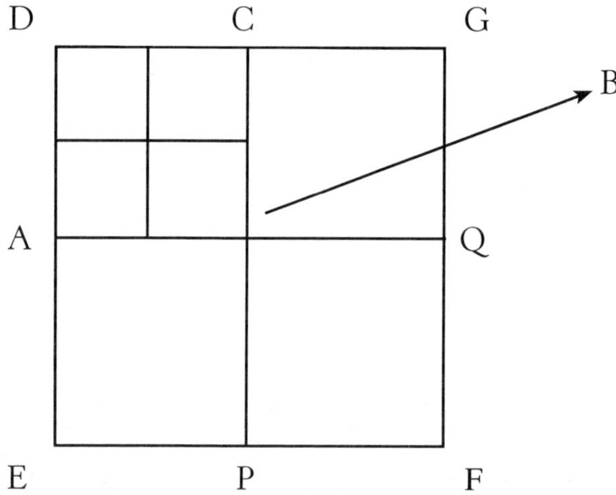

Φ (p. 18) Once the slave realizes that, he knows he needs to look for a line segment between DC and DG, since the former yields an area of 4 square feet, and the later an area of 16 square feet. He then tries a line segment of 3 feet, DZ:

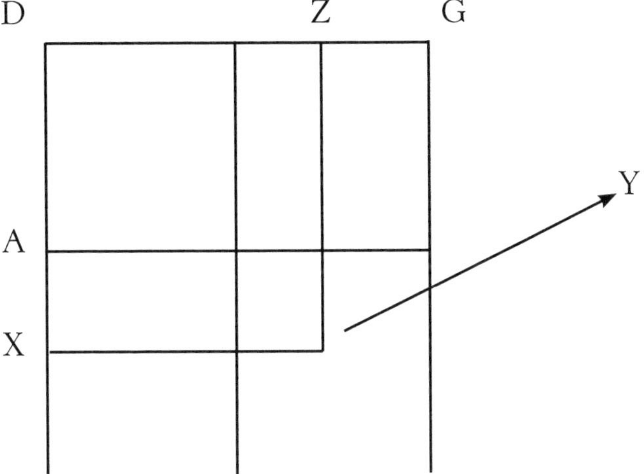

But of course this gives a 9 square feet area DXYZ, which is still too big. At this stage the slave is helpless, as he cannot identify the correct line segment that can produce an area of eight square feet. Yet the slave has made great progress: now at least he knows that he doesn't know!

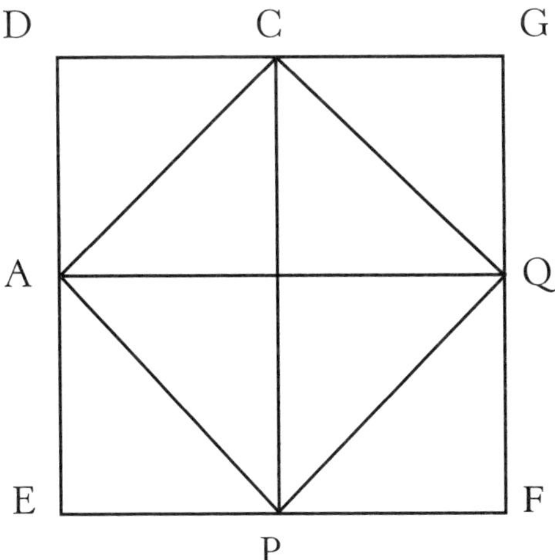

In the final stage Socrates returns to the diagram DEFG, and creates a new square inside it, APQC:

Ψ (p. 19) The four diagonals AP; PQ; QC; CA dissect each inner square to half, hence the total area they create is half the area of DEFG. This area, as the slave has already discovered earlier, is 16 square feet, hence APQC, with an area of 8 square feet, is the sought for square. The line segment that creates it is thus the diagonal AP.

PARMENIDES

Parmenides

Persons of the Dialogue: Cephalus, Adeimantus, Glaucon, Antiphon, Pythodorus, Socrates, Zeno, Parmenides, Aristoteles.

Cephalus rehearses a dialogue which is supposed to have been narrated in his presence by Antiphon, the half-brother of Adeimantus and Glaucon, to certain Clazomenians.

We had come from our home at Clazomenae to Athens, and met 126a
Adeimantus and Glaucon in the Agora. Welcome, Cephalus, said Adeimantus, taking me by the hand; is there anything which we can do for you in Athens?

Yes; that is why I am here; I wish to ask a favor of you.

What may that be? He said.

I want you to tell me the name of your half brother, which I have b
forgotten; he was a mere child when I last came hither from Clazomenae, but that was a long time ago; his father's name, if I remember rightly, was Pyrilampes?

Yes, he said, and the name of our brother, Antiphon; but why do you ask?

Let me introduce some countrymen of mine, I said; they are lovers of philosophy, and have heard that Antiphon was intimate with a certain
Pythodorus, a friend of Zeno, and remembers a conversation which took c
place between Socrates, Zeno, and Parmenides many years ago, Pythodorus having often recited it to him.

Quite true.

And could we hear it? I asked.

Nothing easier, he replied; when he was a youth he made a careful study of the piece; at present his thoughts run in another direction; like his grandfather Antiphon he is devoted to horses. But, if that is what you want, let us go and look for him; he dwells at Melita, which is quite near, and he has only just left us to go home.

127a Accordingly we went to look for him; he was at home, and in the act of
giving a bridle to a smith to be fitted. When he had done with the smith,
his brothers told him the purpose of our visit; and he saluted me as an
acquaintance whom he remembered from my former visit, and we asked
him to repeat the dialogue. At first he was not very willing, and complained
of the trouble, but at length he consented. He told us that Pythodorus had
b described to him the appearance of Parmenides and Zeno; they came to
Athens, as he said, at the great Panathenaea; the former was, at the time of
his visit, about 65 years old, very white with age, but well favored. Zeno
was nearly 40 years of age, tall and fair to look upon; in the days of his
youth he was reported to have been beloved by Parmenides. He said that
they lodged with Pythodorus in the Ceramicus, outside the wall, whither
Socrates, then a very young man, came to see them, and many others with
c him; they wanted to hear the writings of Zeno, which had been brought to
Athens for the first time on the occasion of their visit. These Zeno himself
d read to them in the absence of Parmenides, and had very nearly finished
when Pythodorus entered, and with him Parmenides and Aristoteles who
was afterwards one of the Thirty, and heard the little that remained of the
dialogue. Pythodorus had heard Zeno repeat them before.

When the recitation was completed, Socrates requested that the first
thesis of the first argument might be read over again, and this having been
e done, he said: What is your meaning, Zeno? Do you maintain that if being
is many, it must be both like and unlike, and that this is impossible, for
neither can the like be unlike, nor the unlike like—is that your position?

Just so, said Zeno.

And if the unlike cannot be like, or the like unlike, then according to
you, being could not be many; for this would involve an impossibility. In
all that you say have you any other purpose except to disprove the being
of the many? And is not each division of your treatise intended to furnish
a separate proof of this, there being in all as many proofs of the not-being
of the many as you have composed arguments? Is that your meaning, or
128a have I misunderstood you?

No, said Zeno; you have correctly understood my general purpose.

I see, Parmenides, said Socrates, that Zeno would like to be not only one with you in friendship but your second self in his writings too; he puts what you say in another way, and would fain make believe that he is telling us something which is new. For you, in your poems, say The All is one, and of this you adduce excellent proofs; and he on the other hand says There
is no many; and on behalf of this he offers overwhelming evidence. You b
affirm unity, he denies plurality. And so you deceive the world into believing that you are saying different things when really you are saying much the same. This is a strain of art beyond the reach of most of us.

Yes, Socrates, said Zeno. But although you are as keen as a Spartan c
hound in pursuing the track, you do not fully apprehend the true motive of the composition, which is not really such an artificial work as you imagine; for what you speak of was an accident; there was no pretence of a great purpose; nor any serious intention of deceiving the world. The truth is, that these writings of mine were meant to protect the arguments of
Parmenides against those who make fun of him and seek to show the d
many ridiculous and contradictory results which they suppose to follow from the affirmation of the one. My answer is addressed to the partisans of the many, whose attack I return with interest by retorting upon them that their hypothesis of the being of many, if carried out, appears to be still more ridiculous than the hypothesis of the being of one. Zeal for my master led me to write the book in the days of my youth, but someone
stole the copy; and therefore I had no choice whether it should be pub- e
lished or not; the motive, however, of writing, was not the ambition of an elder man, but the pugnacity of a young one. This you do not seem to see, Socrates; though in other respects, as I was saying, your notion is a very just one.

I understand, said Socrates, and quite accept your account. But tell me, Zeno, do you not further think that there is an idea of likeness in
itself, and another idea of unlikeness, which is the opposite of likeness, 129a
and that in these two, you and I and all other things to which we apply the term many, participate—things which participate in likeness become in that degree and manner like; and so far as they participate in unlikeness become in that degree unlike, or both like and unlike in the degree in which they participate in both? And may not all things partake of both opposites, and be both like and unlike, by reason of this participation?
Where is the wonder? Now if a person could prove the absolute like to b
become unlike, or the absolute unlike to become like, that, in my opinion, would indeed be a wonder; but there is nothing extraordinary, Zeno,

in showing that the things which only partake of likeness and unlikeness
experience both. Nor, again, if a person were to show that all is one by
partaking of one, and at the same time many by partaking of many,
would that be very astonishing. But if he were to show me that the abso-
c lute one was many, or the absolute many one, I should be truly amazed.
And so of all the rest: I should be surprised to hear that the natures or
ideas themselves had these opposite qualities; but not if a person wanted
to prove of me that I was many and also one. When he wanted to show
that I was many he would say that I have a right and a left side, and a front
and a back, and an upper and a lower half, for I cannot deny that I partake of multitude; when, on the other hand, he wants to prove that I am
one, he will say, that we who are here assembled are seven, and that I
d am one and partake of the one. In both instances he proves his case. So
again, if a person shows that such things as wood, stones, and the like,
being many are also one, we admit that he shows the coexistence of the
one and many, but he does not show that the many are one or the one
many; he is uttering not a paradox but a truism. If however, as I just
now suggested, someone were to abstract simple notions of like, unlike,
one, many, rest, motion, and similar ideas, and then to show that these
e admit of admixture and separation in themselves, I should be very much
astonished. This part of the argument appears to be treated by you, Zeno,
in a very spirited manner; but, as I was saying, I should be far more
130a amazed if anyone found in the ideas themselves which are apprehended
by reason, the same puzzle and entanglement which you have shown to
exist in visible objects.

While Socrates was speaking, Pythodorus thought that Parmenides and Zeno were not altogether pleased at the successive steps of the argument; but still they gave the closest attention, and often looked at one another, and smiled as if in admiration of him. When he had finished, Parmenides expressed their feelings in the following words:

b Socrates, he said, I admire the bent of your mind towards philosophy;
tell me now, was this your own distinction between ideas in themselves
and the things which partake of them? And do you think that there is an
idea of likeness apart from the likeness which we possess, and of the one
and many, and of the other things which Zeno mentioned?

I think that there are such ideas, said Socrates.

Parmenides proceeded: And would you also make absolute ideas of the just and the beautiful and the good, and of all that class?

Yes, he said, I should.

And would you make an idea of man apart from us and from all other c
human creatures, or of fire and water?

I am often undecided, Parmenides, as to whether I ought to include them or not.

And would you feel equally undecided, Socrates, about things of which
the mention may provoke a smile? I mean such things as hair, mud, dirt,
or anything else which is vile and paltry; would you suppose that each of d
these has an idea distinct from the actual objects with which we come into
contact, or not?

Certainly not, said Socrates; visible things like these are such as they appear to us, and I am afraid that there would be an absurdity in assuming any idea of them, although I sometimes get disturbed, and begin to think that there is nothing without an idea; but then again, when I have taken up this position, I run away, because I am afraid that I may fall into a bottomless pit of nonsense, and perish; and so I return to the ideas of which I was just now speaking, and occupy myself with them.

Yes, Socrates, said Parmenides; that is because you are still young; the e
time will come, if I am not mistaken, when philosophy will have a firmer
grasp of you, and then you will not despise even the meanest things; at
your age, you are too much disposed to regard the opinions of men. But
I should like to know whether you mean that there are certain ideas of
which all other things partake, and from which they derive their names;
that similars, for example, become similar, because they partake of simi- 131a
larity; and great things become great, because they partake of greatness;
and that just and beautiful things become just and beautiful, because they
partake of justice and beauty?

Yes, certainly, said Socrates that is my meaning.

Then each individual partakes either of the whole of the idea or else of a part of the idea? Can there be any other mode of participation?

There cannot be, he said.

Then do you think that the whole idea is one, and yet, being one, is in each one of the many?

Why not, Parmenides? Said Socrates.

Because one and the same thing will exist as a whole at the same time b
in many separate individuals, and will therefore be in a state of separation
from itself.

Nay, but the idea may be like the day which is one and the same in many places at once, and yet continuous with itself; in this way each idea may be one and the same in all at the same time.

I like your way, Socrates, of making one in many places at once. You mean to say, that if I were to spread out a sail and cover a number of men, there would be one whole including many—is not that your meaning?

c I think so.

And would you say that the whole sail includes each man, or a part of it only, and different parts different men?

The latter.

Then, Socrates, the ideas themselves will be divisible, and things which participate in them will have a part of them only and not the whole idea existing in each of them?

That seems to follow.

Then would you like to say, Socrates, that the one idea is really divisible and yet remains one?

Certainly not, he said.

Suppose that you divide absolute greatness, and that of the many great things, each one is great in virtue of a portion of greatness less than absolute greatness—is that conceivable?

No.

Or will each equal thing, if possessing some small portion of equality
d less than absolute equality, be equal to some other thing by virtue of that portion only?

Impossible.

Or suppose one of us to have a portion of smallness; this is but a part
e of the small, and therefore the absolutely small is greater; if the absolutely small be greater, that to which the part of the small is added will be smaller and not greater than before.

How absurd!

Then in what way, Socrates, will all things participate in the ideas, if they are unable to participate in them either as parts or wholes?

Indeed, he said, you have asked a question which is not easily answered.

Well, said Parmenides, and what do you say of another question?

What question?

132a I imagine that the way in which you are led to assume one idea of each kind is as follows: You see a number of great objects, and when you look at them there seems to you to be one and the same idea (or nature) in them all; hence you conceive of greatness as one.

Very true, said Socrates.

And if you go on and allow your mind in like manner to embrace in one view the idea of greatness and of great things which are not the idea, and to compare them, will not another greatness arise, which will appear to be the source of all these?

It would seem so.

Then another idea of greatness now comes into view over and above absolute greatness, and the individuals which partake of it; and then
another, over and above all these, by virtue of which they will all be great, b
and so each idea instead of being one will be infinitely multiplied.

But may not the ideas, asked Socrates, be thoughts only, and have no proper existence except in our minds, Parmenides? For in that case each idea may still be one, and not experience this infinite multiplication.

And can there be individual thoughts which are thoughts of nothing?

Impossible, he said.

The thought must be of something?

Yes.

Of something which is or which is not? c

Of something which is.

Must it not be of a single something, which the thought recognizes as attaching to all, being a single form or nature?

Yes.

And will not the something which is apprehended as one and the same in all, be an idea?

From that, again, there is no escape.

Then, said Parmenides, if you say that everything else participates in the ideas, must you not say either that everything is made up of thoughts, and that all things think; or that they are thoughts but have no thought?

The latter view, Parmenides, is no more rational than the previous d
one. In my opinion, the ideas are, as it were, patterns fixed in nature, and other things are like them, and resemblances of them—what is meant by the participation of other things in the ideas, is really assimilation to them.

But if, said he, the individual is like the idea, must not the idea also
be like the individual, insofar as the individual is a resemblance of the
idea? That which is like, cannot be conceived of as other than the like e
of like.

Impossible.

And when two things are alike, must they not partake of the same idea?

They must.

And will not that of which the two partake, and which makes them 133a
alike, be the idea itself?

Certainly.

Then the idea cannot be like the individual, or the individual like the idea; for if they are alike, some further idea of likeness will always be coming to light, and if that be like anything else, another; and new ideas will be always arising, if the idea resembles that which partakes of it?

Quite true.

The theory, then, that other things participate in the ideas by resemblance, has to be given up, and some other mode of participation devised?

It would seem so.

Do you see then, Socrates, how great is the difficulty of affirming the ideas to be absolute?

Yes, indeed.

b And, further, let me say that as yet you only understand a small part of the difficulty which is involved if you make of each thing a single idea, parting it off from other things.

What difficulty? He said.

There are many, but the greatest of all is this: If an opponent argues
that these ideas, being such as we say they ought to be, must remain
unknown, no one can prove to him that he is wrong, unless he who denies
their existence be a man of great ability and knowledge, and is willing to
c follow a long and laborious demonstration; he will remain unconvinced,
and still insist that they cannot be known.

What do you mean, Parmenides? Said Socrates.

In the first place, I think, Socrates, that you, or anyone who maintains the existence of absolute essences, will admit that they cannot exist in us.

No, said Socrates; for then they would be no longer absolute.

True, he said; and therefore when ideas are what they are in relation
to one another, their essence is determined by a relation among themselves, and has nothing to do with the resemblances, or whatever they are
to be termed, which are in our sphere, and from which we receive this or
that name when we partake of them. And the things which are within our
d sphere and have the same names with them, are likewise only relative to
one another, and not to the ideas which have the same names with them,
but belong to themselves and not to them.

What do you mean? Said Socrates.

I may illustrate my meaning in this way, said Parmenides: A master has
e a slave; now there is nothing absolute in the relation between them,
which is simply a relation of one man to another. But there is also an idea
of mastership in the abstract, which is relative to the idea of slavery in the

abstract. These natures have nothing to do with us, nor we with them;
they are concerned with themselves only, and we with ourselves. Do you 134a
see my meaning?

Yes, said Socrates, I quite see your meaning.

And will not knowledge—I mean absolute knowledge—answer to absolute truth?

Certainly.

And each kind of absolute knowledge will answer to each kind of absolute being?

Yes.

But the knowledge which we have, will answer to the truth which we
have; and again, each kind of knowledge which we have, will be a knowl- b
edge of each kind of being which we have?

Certainly.

But the ideas themselves, as you admit, we have not, and cannot have?

No, we cannot.

And the absolute natures or kinds are known severally by the absolute idea of knowledge?

Yes.

And we have not got the idea of knowledge?

No.

Then none of the ideas are known to us, because we have no share in absolute knowledge?

I suppose not.

Then the nature of the beautiful in itself, and of the good in itself, and c
all other ideas which we suppose to exist absolutely, are unknown to us?

It would seem so.

I think that there is a stranger consequence still.

What is it?

Would you, or would you not say, that absolute knowledge, if there is such a thing, must be a far more exact knowledge than our knowledge; and the same of beauty and of the rest?

Yes.

And if there be such a thing as participation in absolute knowledge, no one is more likely than God to have this most exact knowledge?

Certainly.

But then, will God, having absolute knowledge, have a knowledge of d
human things?

Why not?

Because, Socrates, said Parmenides, we have admitted that the ideas are not valid in relation to human things; nor human things in relation to them; the relations of either are limited to their respective spheres.

Yes, that has been admitted.

And if God has this perfect authority, and perfect knowledge, his
e authority cannot rule us, nor his knowledge know us, or any human thing; just as our authority does not extend to the gods, nor our knowledge know anything which is divine, so by parity of reason they, being gods, are not our masters, neither do they know the things of men.

Yet, surely, said Socrates, to deprive God of knowledge is monstrous.

135a These, Socrates, said Parmenides, are a few, and only a few of the difficulties in which we are involved if ideas really are and we determine each one of them to be an absolute unity. He who hears what may be said against them will deny the very existence of them—and even if they do exist, he will say that they must of necessity be unknown to man; and he will seem to have reason on his side, and as we were remarking just now, will be very difficult to convince; a man must be gifted with very considerable ability before he can learn that everything has a class and an
b absolute essence; and still more remarkable will he be who discovers all these things for himself, and having thoroughly investigated them is able to teach them to others.

I agree with you, Parmenides, said Socrates; and what you say is very much to my mind.

And yet, Socrates, said Parmenides, if a man, fixing his attention on these and the like difficulties, does away with ideas of things and will not
c admit that every individual thing has its own determinate idea which is always one and the same, he will have nothing on which his mind can rest; and so he will utterly destroy the power of reasoning, as you seem to me to have particularly noted.

Very true, he said.

But, then, what is to become of philosophy? Whither shall we turn, if the ideas are unknown?

I certainly do not see my way at present.

Yes, said Parmenides; and I think that this arises, Socrates, out of your attempting to define the beautiful, the just, the good, and the ideas
d generally, without sufficient previous training. I noticed your deficiency, when I heard you talking here with your friend Aristoteles, the day before yesterday. The impulse that carries you towards philosophy is assuredly noble and divine; but there is an art which is called by the

vulgar idle talking, and which is often imagined to be useless; in that you must train and exercise yourself, now that you are young, or truth will elude your grasp.

And what is the nature of this exercise, Parmenides, which you would recommend?

That which you heard Zeno practicing; at the same time, I give you
credit for saying to him that you did not care to examine the perplexity e
in reference to visible things, or to consider the question that way; but
only in reference to objects of thought, and to what may be called ideas.

Why, yes, he said, there appears to me to be no difficulty in showing by this method that visible things are like and unlike and may experience anything.

Quite true, said Parmenides; but I think that you should go a step
further, and consider not only the consequences which flow from a given 136a
hypothesis, but also the consequences which flow from denying the hypothesis; and that will be still better training for you.

What do you mean? He said.

I mean, for example, that in the case of this very hypothesis of Zeno's
about the many, you should inquire not only what will be the consequences to the many in relation to themselves and to the one, and to the
one in relation to itself and the many, on the hypothesis of the being of
the many, but also what will be the consequences to the one and the many
in their relation to themselves and to each other, on the opposite hypothesis. Or, again, if likeness is or is not, what will be the consequences in
either of these cases to the subjects of the hypothesis, and to other things, b
in relation both to themselves and to one another, and so of unlikeness;
and the same holds good of motion and rest, of generation and destruction, and even of being and not-being. In a word, when you suppose
anything to be or not to be, or to be in any way affected, you must look c
at the consequences in relation to the thing itself, and to any other things
which you choose—to each of them singly, to more than one, and to all;
and so of other things, you must look at them in relation to themselves and
to anything else which you suppose either to be or not to be, if you would
train yourself perfectly and see the real truth.

That, Parmenides, is a tremendous business of which you speak, and I do not quite understand you; will you take some hypothesis and go through the steps? Then I shall apprehend you better.

That, Socrates, is a serious task to impose on a man of my years. d

Then will you, Zeno? Said Socrates.

Zeno answered with a smile: Let us make our petition to Parmenides
himself, who is quite right in saying that you are hardly aware of the extent
of the task which you are imposing on him; and if there were more of us
I should not ask him, for these are not subjects which anyone, especially
e at his age, can well speak of before a large audience; most people are not
aware that this roundabout progress through all things is the only way in
which the mind can attain truth and wisdom. And therefore, Parmenides,
I join in the request of Socrates, that I may hear the process again which I
have not heard for a long time.

When Zeno had thus spoken, Pythodorus, according to Antiphon's
report of him, said, that he himself and Aristoteles and the whole company
entreated Parmenides to give an example of the process. I cannot refuse,
said Parmenides; and yet I feel rather like Ibycus, who, when in his old age,
against his will, he fell in love, compared himself to an old racehorse, who
was about to run in a chariot race, shaking with fear at the course he knew
137a so well—this was his simile of himself. And I also experience a trembling
when I remember through what an ocean of words I have to wade at my
time of life. But I must indulge you, as Zeno says that I ought, and we are
b alone. Where shall I begin? And what shall be our first hypothesis, if I am
to attempt this laborious pastime? Shall I begin with myself, and take my
own hypothesis the one? And consider the consequences which follow on
the supposition either of the being or of the not-being of one?

By all means, said Zeno.

And who will answer me? He said. Shall I propose the youngest? He will not make difficulties and will be the most likely to say what he thinks; and his answers will give me time to breathe.

c I am the one whom you mean, Parmenides, said Aristoteles; for I am
the youngest and at your service. Ask, and I will answer.

Parmenides proceeded: 1.a. If one is, he said, the one cannot be many?

Impossible.

Then the one cannot have parts, and cannot be a whole?

Why not?

Because every part is part of a whole; is it not?

Yes.

And what is a whole? Would not that of which no part is wanting be a whole?

Certainly.

Then, in either case, the one would be made up of parts; both as being a whole, and also as having parts?

To be sure.

And in either case, the one would be many, and not one?

True. d

But, surely, it ought to be one and not many?

It ought.

Then, if the one is to remain one, it will not be a whole, and will not have parts?

No.

But if it has no parts, it will have neither beginning, middle, nor end; for these would of course be parts of it.

Right.

But then, again, a beginning and an end are the limits of everything?

Certainly.

Then the one, having neither beginning nor end, is unlimited?

Yes, unlimited.

And therefore formless; for it cannot partake either of round or straight.

But why? e

Why, because the round is that of which all the extreme points are equidistant from the center?

Yes.

And the straight is that of which the center intercepts the view of the extremes?

True.

Then the one would have parts and would be many, if it partook either of a straight or of a circular form?

Assuredly.

But having no parts, it will be neither straight nor round? 138a

Right.

And, being of such a nature, it cannot be in any place, for it cannot be either in another or in itself.

How so?

Because if it were in another, it would be encircled by that in which it was, and would touch it at many places and with many parts; but that which is one and indivisible, and does not partake of a circular nature, cannot be touched all round in many places.

Certainly not.

But if, on the other hand, one were in itself, it would also be contained
by nothing else but itself; that is to say, if it were really in itself; for nothing b
can be in anything which does not contain it.

Impossible.

But then, that which contains must be other than that which is contained? For the same whole cannot do and suffer both at once; and if so, one will be no longer one, but two?

True.

Then one cannot be anywhere, either in itself or in another?

No.

Further consider, whether that which is of such a nature can have either rest or motion.

Why not?

Why, because the one, if it were moved, would be either moved in place or changed in nature; for these are the only kinds of motion.

c Yes.

And the one, when it changes and ceases to be itself, cannot be any longer one.

It cannot.

It cannot therefore experience the sort of motion which is change of nature?

Clearly not.

Then can the motion of the one be in place?

Perhaps.

But if the one moved in place, must it not either move round and round in the same place, or from one place to another?

It must.

And that which moves in a circle must rest upon a center; and that which goes round upon a center must have parts which are different from
d the center; but that which has no center and no parts cannot possibly be carried round upon a center?

Impossible.

But perhaps the motion of the one consists in change of place?

Perhaps so, if it moves at all.

And have we not already shown that it cannot be in anything?

Yes.

Then its coming into being in anything is still more impossible; is it not?

I do not see why.

Why, because anything which comes into being in anything, can neither as yet be in that other thing while still coming into being, nor be altogether out of it, if already coming into being in it.

Certainly not.

And therefore whatever comes into being in another must have parts, e
and then one part may be in, and another part out of that other; but that which has no parts can never be at one and the same time neither wholly within nor wholly without anything.

True.

And is there not a still greater impossibility in that which has no parts, 139a
and is not a whole, coming into being anywhere, since it cannot come into being either as a part or as a whole?

Clearly.

Then it does not change place by revolving in the same spot, nor by going somewhere and coming into being in something; nor again, by change in itself?

Very true.

Then in respect of any kind of motion the one is immoveable?

Immoveable.

But neither can the one be in anything, as we affirm?

Yes, we said so.

Then it is never in the same?

Why not?

Because if it were in the same it would be in something.

Certainly.

And we said that it could not be in itself, and could not be in other?

True.

Then one is never in the same place?

It would seem not.

But that which is never in the same place is never quiet or at rest? b

Never.

One then, as would seem, is neither at rest nor in motion?

It certainly appears so.

Neither will it be the same with itself or other; nor again, other than itself or other.

How is that?

If other than itself it would be other than one, and would not be one.

True.

And if the same with other, it would be that other, and not itself; so
that upon this supposition too, it would not have the nature of one, but c
would be other than one?

It would.

Then it will not be the same with other, or other than itself?

It will not.

Neither will it be other than other, while it remains one; for not one, but only other, can be other than other, and nothing else.

True.

Then not by virtue of being one will it be other?

Certainly not.

But if not by virtue of being one, not by virtue of itself; and if not by virtue of itself, not itself, and itself not being other at all, will not be other than anything?

d Right.

Neither will one be the same with itself.

How not?

Surely the nature of the one is not the nature of the same.

Why not?

It is not when anything becomes the same with anything that it becomes one.

What of that?

Anything which becomes the same with the many, necessarily becomes many and not one.

True.

But, if there were no difference between the one and the same, when a thing became the same, it would always become one; and when it became one, the same?

e Certainly.

And, therefore, if one be the same with itself, it is not one with itself, and will therefore be one and also not one.

Surely that is impossible.

And therefore the one can neither be other than other, nor the same with itself.

Impossible.

And thus the one can neither be the same, nor other, either in relation to itself or other?

No.

Neither will the one be like anything or unlike itself or other.

Why not?

Because likeness is sameness of affections.

Yes.

140a And sameness has been shown to be of a nature distinct from oneness?

That has been shown.

But if the one had any other affection than that of being one, it would be affected in such a way as to be more than one; which is impossible.

True. b

Then the one can never be so affected as to be the same either with another or with itself?

Clearly not.

Then it cannot be like another, or like itself?

No.

Nor can it be affected so as to be other, for then it would be affected c
in such a way as to be more than one.

It would.

That which is affected otherwise than itself or another, will be unlike itself or another, for sameness of affections is likeness.

True.

But the one, as appears, never being affected otherwise, is never unlike itself or other?

Never.

Then the one will never be either like or unlike itself or other?

Plainly not.

Again, being of this nature, it can neither be equal nor unequal either to itself or to other.

How is that?

Why, because the one if equal must be of the same measures as that to which it is equal.

True.

And if greater or less than things which are commensurable with it, the one will have more measures than that which is less, and fewer than that which is greater?

Yes.

And so of things which are not commensurate with it, the one will have greater measures than that which is less and smaller than that which is greater.

Certainly.

But how can that which does not partake of sameness, have either the same measures or have anything else the same?

Impossible.

And not having the same measures, the one cannot be equal either with itself or with another?

It appears so.

d But again, whether it have fewer or more measures, it will have as many parts as it has measures; and thus again the one will be no longer one but will have as many parts as measures.

Right.

And if it were of one measure, it would be equal to that measure; yet it has been shown to be incapable of equality.

It has.

Then it will neither partake of one measure, nor of many, nor of few, nor of the same at all, nor be equal to itself or another; nor be greater or less than itself, or other?

Certainly.

e Well, and do we suppose that one can be older, or younger than anything, or of the same age with it?

Why not?

Why, because that which is of the same age with itself or other, must partake of equality or likeness of time; and we said that the one did not partake either of equality or of likeness?

We did say so.

And we also said, that it did not partake of inequality or unlikeness.

Very true.

141a How then can one, being of this nature, be either older or younger than anything, or have the same age with it?

In no way.

Then one cannot be older or younger, or of the same age, either with itself or with another?

Clearly not.

Then the one, being of this nature, cannot be in time at all; for must not that which is in time, be always growing older than itself?

Certainly.

And that which is older, must always be older than something which is younger?

True.

b Then, that which becomes older than itself, also becomes at the same time younger than itself, if it is to have something to become older than.

What do you mean?

I mean this: A thing does not need to become different from another thing which is already different; it IS different, and if its different has become, it has become different; if its different will be, it will be different;

but of that which is becoming different, there cannot have been, or be about to be, or yet be, a different—the only different possible is one which is becoming.

That is inevitable. c

But, surely, the elder is a difference relative to the younger, and to nothing else.

True.

Then that which becomes older than itself must also, at the same time, become younger than itself?

Yes.

But again, it is true that it cannot become for a longer or for a shorter time than itself, but it must become, and be, and have become, and be d
about to be, for the same time with itself?

That again is inevitable.

Then things which are in time, and partake of time, must in every case, I suppose, be of the same age with themselves; and must also become at once older and younger than themselves?

Yes.

But the one did not partake of those affections?

Not at all.

Then it does not partake of time, and is not in any time?

So the argument shows.

Well, but do not the expressions "was," and "has become," and "was becoming," signify a participation of past time?

Certainly.

And do not "will be," "will become," "will have become," signify a par- e
ticipation of future time?

Yes.

And "is," or "becomes," signifies a participation of present time?

Certainly.

And if the one is absolutely without participation in time, it never had become, or was becoming, or was at any time, or is now become or is becoming, or is, or will become, or will have become, or will be, hereafter.

Most true.

But are there any modes of partaking of being other than these?

There are none.

Then the one cannot possibly partake of being?

That is the inference.

Then the one is not at all?

Clearly not.

Then the one does not exist in such way as to be one; for if it were and partook of being, it would already be; but if the argument is to be trusted, the one neither is nor is one?

142a True.

But that which is not admits of no attribute or relation?

Of course not.

Then there is no name, nor expression, nor perception, nor opinion, nor knowledge of it?

Clearly not.

Then it is neither named, nor expressed, nor opined, nor known, nor does anything that is perceive it.

So we must infer.

But can all this be true about the one?

I think not.

b 1.b. Suppose, now, that we return once more to the original hypothesis; let us see whether, on a further review, any new aspect of the question appears.

I shall be very happy to do so.

We say that we have to work out together all the consequences, whatever they may be, which follow, if the one is?

Yes.

Then we will begin at the beginning: If one is, can one be, and not partake of being?

Impossible.

Then the one will have being, but its being will not be the same with the one; for if the same, it would not be the being of the one; nor would the
c one have participated in being, for the proposition that one is would have been identical with the proposition that one is one; but our hypothesis is not if one is one, what will follow, but if one is: am I not right?

Quite right.

We mean to say, that being has not the same significance as one?

Of course.

And when we put them together shortly, and say "One is," that is equivalent to saying, "partakes of being"?

Quite true.

Once more then let us ask, if one is what will follow. Does not this hypothesis necessarily imply that one is of such a nature as to have parts?

d How so?

In this way: If being is predicated of the one, if the one is, and one of being, if being is one; and if being and one are not the same; and since the one, which we have assumed, is, must not the whole, if it is one, itself be, and have for its parts, one and being?

Certainly.

And is each of these parts—one and being—to be simply called a part, or must the word "part" be relative to the word "whole"?

The latter.

Then that which is one is both a whole and has a part?

Certainly.

Again, of the parts of the one, if it is—I mean being and one—does e
either fail to imply the other? Is the one wanting to being, or being to the one?

Impossible.

Thus, each of the parts also has in turn both one and being, and is at the least made up of two parts; and the same principle goes on forever, and every part whatever has always these two parts; for being always involves one, and one being; so that one is always disappearing, and becoming two.

Certainly. 143a

And so the one, if it is, must be infinite in multiplicity?

Clearly.

Let us take another direction.

What direction?

We say that the one partakes of being and therefore it is?

Yes.

And in this way, the one, if it has being, has turned out to be many?

True.

But now, let us abstract the one which, as we say, partakes of being, and try to imagine it apart from that of which, as we say, it partakes—will this abstract one be one only or many?

One, I think.

Let us see: Must not the being of one be other than one? For the one b
is not being, but, considered as one, only partook of being?

Certainly.

If being and the one be two different things, it is not because the one is one that it is other than being; nor because being is being that it is other than the one; but they differ from one another in virtue of otherness and difference.

Certainly.

So that the other is not the same—either with the one or with being?

Certainly not.

c And therefore whether we take being and the other, or being and the one, or the one and the other, in every such case we take two things, which may be rightly called both.

How so.

In this way—you may speak of being?

Yes.

And also of one?

Yes.

Then now we have spoken of either of them?

Yes.

Well, and when I speak of being and one, I speak of them both?

Certainly.

And if I speak of being and the other, or of the one and the other—in any such case do I not speak of both?

Yes.

d And must not that which is correctly called both, be also two?

Undoubtedly.

And of two things how can either by any possibility not be one?

It cannot.

Then, if the individuals of the pair are together two, they must be severally one?

Clearly.

And if each of them is one, then by the addition of any one to any pair, the whole becomes three?

Yes.

And three are odd, and two are even?

Of course.

e And if there are two there must also be twice, and if there are three there must be thrice; that is, if twice one makes two, and thrice one three?

Certainly.

There are two, and twice, and therefore there must be twice two; and there are three, and there is thrice, and therefore there must be thrice three?

Of course.

If there are three and twice, there is twice three; and if there are two and thrice, there is thrice two?

Undoubtedly.

Here, then, we have even taken even times, and odd taken odd times, and even taken odd times, and odd taken even times. 144a

True.

And if this is so, does any number remain which has no necessity to be?

None whatever.

Then if one is, number must also be?

It must.

But if there is number, there must also be many, and infinite multiplicity of being; for number is infinite in multiplicity, and partakes also of being: am I not right?

Certainly.

And if all number participates in being, every part of number will also participate?

Yes.

Then being is distributed over the whole multitude of things, and nothing b
that is, however small or however great, is devoid of it? And, indeed, the very supposition of this is absurd, for how can that which is, be devoid of being?

In no way.

And it is divided into the greatest and into the smallest, and into being of all sizes, and is broken up more than all things; the divisions of it have no limit.

True. c

Then it has the greatest number of parts?

Yes, the greatest number.

Is there any of these which is a part of being, and yet no part?

Impossible.

But if it is at all and so long as it is, it must be one, and cannot be none?

Certainly.

Then the one attaches to every single part of being, and does not fail in any part, whether great or small, or whatever may be the size of it?

True.

But reflect: Can one, in its entirety, be in many places at the same time? d

No; I see the impossibility of that.

And if not in its entirety, then it is divided; for it cannot be present with all the parts of being, unless divided.

True.

And that which has parts will be as many as the parts are?

Certainly.

Then we were wrong in saying just now, that being was distributed
e into the greatest number of parts. For it is not distributed into parts more than the one, into parts equal to the one; the one is never wanting to being, or being to the one, but being two they are coequal and coextensive.

Certainly that is true.

The one itself, then, having been broken up into parts by being, is many and infinite?

True.

Then not only the one which has being is many, but the one itself distributed by being, must also be many?

Certainly.

Further, inasmuch as the parts are parts of a whole, the one, as a whole, will be limited; for are not the parts contained by the whole?

145a Certainly.

And that which contains, is a limit?

Of course.

Then the one if it has being is one and many, whole and parts, having limits and yet unlimited in number?

Clearly.

And because having limits, also having extremes?

Certainly.

And if a whole, having beginning and middle and end. For can anything be a whole without these three? And if any one of them is wanting to anything, will that any longer be a whole?

No.

b Then the one, as appears, will have beginning, middle, and end.

It will.

But, again, the middle will be equidistant from the extremes; or it would not be in the middle?

Yes.

Then the one will partake of figure, either rectilinear or round, or a union of the two?

True.

And if this is the case, it will be both in itself and in another too.

How?

Every part is in the whole, and none is outside the whole.

True.

And all the parts are contained by the whole?

c Yes.

And the one is all its parts, and neither more nor less than all?

No.

And the one is the whole?

Of course.

But if all the parts are in the whole, and the one is all of them and the whole, and they are all contained by the whole, the one will be contained by the one; and thus the one will be in itself.

That is true.

But then, again, the whole is not in the parts—neither in all the parts,
nor in some one of them. For if it is in all, it must be in one; for if there d
were any one in which it was not, it could not be in all the parts; for the
part in which it is wanting is one of all, and if the whole is not in this, how
can it be in them all?

It cannot.

Nor can the whole be in some of the parts; for if the whole were in some of the parts, the greater would be in the less, which is impossible.

Yes, impossible.

But if the whole is neither in one, nor in more than one, nor in all of the parts, it must be in something else, or cease to be anywhere at all?

Certainly. e

If it were nowhere, it would be nothing; but being a whole, and not being in itself, it must be in another.

Very true.

The one then, regarded as a whole, is in another, but regarded as being all its parts, is in itself; and therefore the one must be itself in itself and also in another.

Certainly.

The one then, being of this nature, is of necessity both at rest and in motion?

How?

The one is at rest since it is in itself, for being in one, and not passing 146a
out of this, it is in the same, which is itself.

True.

And that which is ever in the same, must be ever at rest?

Certainly.

Well, and must not that, on the contrary, which is ever in other, never be in the same; and if never in the same, never at rest, and if not at rest, in motion?

True.

Then the one being always itself in itself and other, must always be both at rest and in motion?

Clearly.

b And must be the same with itself, and other than itself; and also the same with the others, and other than the others; this follows from its previous affections.

How so?

Everything in relation to every other thing, is either the same or other; or if neither the same nor other, then in the relation of a part to a whole, or of a whole to a part.

Clearly.

c And is the one a part of itself?

Certainly not.

Since it is not a part in relation to itself it cannot be related to itself as whole to part?

It cannot.

But is the one other than one?

No.

And therefore not other than itself?

Certainly not.

If then it be neither other, nor a whole, nor a part in relation to itself, must it not be the same with itself?

Certainly.

But then, again, a thing which is in another place from "itself," if this "itself" remains in the same place with itself, must be other than "itself," for it will be in another place?

True.

Then the one has been shown to be at once in itself and in another?

Yes.

Thus, then, as appears, the one will be other than itself?

True.

d Well, then, if anything be other than anything, will it not be other than mat which is other?

Certainly.

And will not all things that are not one, be other than the one, and the one other than the not-one?

Of course.

Then the one will be other than the others?

True.

But, consider: Are not the absolute same, and the absolute other, opposites to one another?

Of course.

Then will the same ever be in the other, or the other in the same?

They will not.

If then the other is never in the same, there is nothing in which the
other is during any space of time; for during that space of time, however e
small, the other would be in the same. Is not that true?

Yes.

And since the other is never in the same, it can never be in anything that is.

True.

Then the other will never be either in the not-one, or in the one?

Certainly not.

Then not by reason of otherness is the one other than the not-one, or the not-one other than the one.

No.

Nor by reason of themselves will they be other than one another, if not partaking of the other.

How can they be? 147a

But if they are not other, either by reason of themselves or of the other, will they not altogether escape being other than one another?

They will.

Again, the not-one cannot partake of the one; otherwise it would not have been not-one, but would have been in some way one.

True.

Nor can the not-one be number; for having number, it would not have been not-one at all.

It would not.

Again, is the not-one part of the one; or rather, would it not in that case partake of the one?

It would.

If then, in every point of view, the one and the not-one are distinct,
then neither is the one part or whole of the not-one, nor is the not-one b
part or whole of the one?

No.

But we said that things which are neither parts nor wholes of one another, nor other than one another, will be the same with one another: so we said?

Yes.

Then shall we say that the one, being in this relation to the not-one, is the same with it?

Let us say so.

Then it is the same with itself and the others, and also other than itself and the others.

That appears to be the inference.

c And it will also be like and unlike itself and the others?

Perhaps.

Since the one was shown to be other than the others, the others will also be other than the one.

Yes.

And the one is other than the others in the same degree that the others are other than it, and neither more nor less?

True.

And if neither more nor less, then in a like degree?

Yes.

In virtue of the affection by which the one is other than others and others in like manner other than it, the one will be affected like the others and the others like the one.

d How do you mean?

I may take as an illustration the case of names: You give a name to a thing?

Yes.

And you may say the name once or oftener?

Yes.

And when you say it once, you mention that of which it is the name? And when more than once, is it something else which you mention? Or must it always be the same thing of which you speak, whether you utter the name once or more than once?

Of course it is the same.

And is not "other" a name given to a thing?

Certainly.

e Whenever, then, you use the word "other," whether once or oftener, you name that of which it is the name, and to no other do you give the name?

True.

Then when we say that the others are other than the one, and the one other than the others, in repeating the word "other" we speak of that nature to which the name is applied, and of no other?

Quite true.

Then the one which is other than others, and the other which is other than the one, in that the word "other" is applied to both, will be in the same condition; and that which is in the same condition is like? 148a

Yes.

Then in virtue of the affection by which the one is other than the others, everything will be like everything, for every thing is other than every thing.

True.

Again, the like is opposed to the unlike?

Yes.

And the other to the same?

True again.

And the one was also shown to be the same with the others?

Yes. b

And to be the same with the others is the opposite of being other than the others?

Certainly.

And in that it was other it was shown to be like?

Yes.

But in that it was the same it will be unlike by virtue of the opposite affection to that which made it like; and this was the affection of otherness.

Yes.

The same then will make it unlike; otherwise it will not be the opposite of the other.

True. c

Then the one will be both like and unlike the others; like insofar as it is other, and unlike insofar as it is the same.

Yes, that argument may be used.

And there is another argument.

What?

Insofar as it is affected in the same way it is not affected otherwise, and not being affected otherwise is not unlike, and not being unlike, is like; but insofar as it is affected by other it is otherwise, and being otherwise affected is unlike.

True.

Then because the one is the same with the others and other than the others, on either of these two grounds, or on both of them, it will be both like and unlike the others?

Certainly. d

And in the same way as being other than itself and the same with itself, on either of these two grounds and on both of them, it will be like and unlike itself?

Of course.

Again, how far can the one touch or not touch itself and others? Consider.

I am considering.

The one was shown to be in itself which was a whole?

True.

And also in other things?

Yes.

e Insofar as it is in other things it would touch other things, but insofar as it is in itself it would be debarred from touching them, and would touch itself only.

Clearly.

Then the inference is that it would touch both?

It would.

But what do you say to a new point of view? Must not that which is to touch another be next to that which it is to touch, and occupy the place nearest to that in which what it touches is situated?

True.

Then the one, if it is to touch itself, ought to be situated next to itself, and occupy the place next to that in which itself is?

It ought.

And that would require that the one should be two, and be in two places at once, and this, while it is one, will never happen.

No.

149a Then the one cannot touch itself any more than it can be two?

It cannot.

Neither can it touch others.

Why not?

The reason is, that whatever is to touch another must be in separation from, and next to, that which it is to touch, and no third thing can be between them.

True.

Two things, then, at the least are necessary to make contact possible?

They are.

And if to the two a third be added in due order, the number of terms will be three, and the contacts two?

Yes.

And every additional term makes one additional contact, whence it b
follows that the contacts are one less in number than the terms; the first two terms exceeded the number of contacts by one, and the whole number of terms exceeds the whole number of contacts by one in like manner; and for every one which is afterwards added to the number of terms, one contact is added to the contacts.

True. c

Whatever is the whole number of things, the contacts will be always one less.

True.

But if there be only one, and not two, there will be no contact?

How can there be?

And do we not say that the others being other than the one are not one and have no part in the one?

True.

Then they have no number, if they have no one in them?

Of course not. d

Then the others are neither one nor two, nor are they called by the name of any number?

No.

One, then, alone is one, and two do not exist?

Clearly not.

And if there are not two, there is no contact?

There is not.

Then neither does the one touch the others, nor the others the one, if there is no contact?

Certainly not.

For all which reasons the one touches and does not touch itself and the others?

True.

Further—is the one equal and unequal to itself and others?

How do you mean?

If the one were greater or less than the others, or the others
greater or less than the one, they would not be greater or less than e
each other in virtue of their being the one and the others; but, if in addition to their being what they are they had equality, they would be equal to one another, or if the one had smallness and the others greatness, or the one had greatness and the others smallness—whichever

kind had greatness would be greater, and whichever had smallness would be smaller?

Certainly.

Then there are two such ideas as greatness and smallness; for if they were not they could not be opposed to each other and be present in that which is.

150a How could they?

If, then, smallness is present in the one it will be present either in the whole or in a part of the whole?

Certainly.

Suppose the first; it will be either coequal and coextensive with the whole one, or will contain the one?

Clearly.

If it be coextensive with the one it will be coequal with the one, or if containing the one it will be greater than the one?

Of course.

But can smallness be equal to anything or greater than anything, and have the functions of greatness and equality and not its own functions?

b Impossible.

Then smallness cannot be in the whole of one, but, if at all, in a part only?

Yes.

And surely not in all of a part, for then the difficulty of the whole will recur; it will be equal to or greater than any part in which it is.

Certainly.

Then smallness will not be in anything, whether in a whole or in a part; nor will there be anything small but actual smallness.

True.

Neither will greatness be in the one, for if greatness be in anything there will be something greater other and besides greatness itself, namely,
c that in which greatness is; and this too when the small itself is not there, which the one, if it is great, must exceed; this, however, is impossible, seeing that smallness is wholly absent.

True.

But absolute greatness is only greater than absolute smallness, and smallness is only smaller than absolute greatness.

Very true.

Then other things not greater or less than the one, if they have neither greatness nor smallness; nor have greatness or smallness any power of exceeding or being exceeded in relation to the one, but only in relation to one another; nor will the one be greater or less than them or others, if it has neither greatness nor smallness.

Clearly not.

Then if the one is neither greater nor less than the others, it cannot d
either exceed or be exceeded by them?

Certainly not.

And that which neither exceeds nor is exceeded, must be on an equality; and being on an equality, must be equal.

Of course.

And this will be true also of the relation of the one to itself; having e
neither greatness nor smallness in itself, it will neither exceed nor be exceeded by itself, but will be on an equality with and equal to itself.

Certainly.

Then the one will be equal both to itself and the others?

Clearly so.

And yet the one, being itself in itself, will also surround and be without itself; and, as containing itself, will be greater than itself; and, as contained in itself, will be less; and will thus be greater and less than itself.

It will. 151a

Now there cannot possibly be anything which is not included in the one and the others?

Of course not.

But, surely, that which is must always be somewhere?

Yes.

But that which is in anything will be less, and that in which it is will be greater; in no other way can one thing be in another.

True. b

And since there is nothing other or besides the one and the others, and they must be in something, must they not be in one another, the one in the others and the others in the one, if they are to be anywhere?

That is clear.

But inasmuch as the one is in the others, the others will be greater than the one, because they contain the one, which will be less than the others, because it is contained in them; and inasmuch as the others are in the one, the one on the same principle will be greater than the others, and the others less than the one.

True.

The one, then, will be equal to and greater and less than itself and the others?

Clearly.

And if it be greater and less and equal, it will be of equal and more and less measures or divisions than itself and the others, and if of measures, also of parts?

c Of course.

And if of equal and more and less measures or divisions, it will be in number more or less than itself and the others, and likewise equal in number to itself and to the others?

How is that?

It will be of more measures than those things which it exceeds, and of as many parts as measures; and so with that to which it is equal, and that than which it is less.

True.

And being greater and less than itself, and equal to itself, it will be of
d equal measures with itself and of more and fewer measures than itself; and if of measures then also of parts?

It will.

And being of equal parts with itself, it will be numerically equal to itself; and being of more parts, more, and being of less, less than itself?

Certainly.

And the same will hold of its relation to other things; inasmuch as it is greater than them, it will be more in number than them; and inasmuch as it is smaller, it will be less in number; and inasmuch as it is equal in size to other things, it will be equal to them in number.

Certainly.

e Once more, then, as would appear, the one will be in number both equal to and more and less than both itself and all other things.

It will.

Does the one also partake of time? And is it and does it become older and younger than itself and others, and again, neither younger nor older than itself and others, by virtue of participation in time?

How do you mean?

If one is, being must be predicated of it?

Yes.

152a But to be (einai) is only participation of being in present time, and to have been is the participation of being at a past time, and to be about to be is the participation of being at a future time?

Very true.

Then the one, since it partakes of being, partakes of time?

Certainly.

And is not time always moving forward?

Yes.

Then the one is always becoming older than itself, since it moves forward in time?

Certainly. b

And do you remember that the older becomes older than that which becomes younger?

I remember.

Then since the one becomes older than itself, it becomes younger at the same time?

Certainly.

Thus, then, the one becomes older as well as younger than itself?

Yes.

And it is older (is it not?) when in becoming, it gets to the point of time between "was" and "will be," which is "now": for surely in going from the past to the future, it cannot skip the present?

No.

And when it arrives at the present it stops from becoming older, and
no longer becomes, but is older, for if it went on it would never be c
reached by the present, for it is the nature of that which goes on, to touch both the present and the future, letting go the present and seizing the future, while in process of becoming between them.

True.

But that which is becoming cannot skip the present; when it reaches
the present it ceases to become, and is then whatever it may happen to d
be becoming.

Clearly.

And so the one, when in becoming older it reaches the present, ceases to become, and is then older.

Certainly.

And it is older than that than which it was becoming older, and it was becoming older than itself.

Yes.

And that which is older is older than that which is younger?

True.

Then the one is younger than itself, when in becoming older it reaches the present?

Certainly.

e But the present is always present with the one during all its being; for whenever it is it is always now.

Certainly.

Then the one always both is and becomes older and younger than itself?

Truly.

And is it or does it become a longer time than itself or an equal time with itself?

An equal time.

But if it becomes or is for an equal time with itself, it is of the same age with itself?

Of course.

And that which is of the same age, is neither older nor younger?

No.

The one, then, becoming and being the same time with itself, neither is nor becomes older or younger than itself?

I should say not.

And what are its relations to other things? Is it or does it become older or younger than they?

I cannot tell you.

153a You can at least tell me that others than the one are more than the one—other would have been one, but the others have multitude, and are more than one?

They will have multitude.

And a multitude implies a number larger than one?

Of course.

And shall we say that the lesser or the greater is the first to come or to have come into existence?

The lesser.

Then the least is the first? And that is the one?

b Yes.

Then the one of all things that have number is the first to come into being; but all other things have also number, being plural and not singular.

They have.

And since it came into being first it must be supposed to have come into being prior to the others, and the others later; and the things which came into being later, are younger than that which preceded them? And so the other things will be younger than the one, and the one older than other things?

True.

What would you say of another question? Can the one have come into being contrary to its own nature, or is that impossible?

Impossible. c

And yet, surely, the one was shown to have parts; and if parts, then a beginning, middle and end?

Yes.

And a beginning, both of the one itself and of all other things, comes into being first of all; and after the beginning, the others follow, until you reach the end?

Certainly.

And all these others we shall affirm to be parts of the whole and of the one, which, as soon as the end is reached, has become whole and one?

Yes; that is what we shall say.

But the end comes last, and the one is of such a nature as to come into d
being with the last; and, since the one cannot come into being except in accordance with its own nature, its nature will require that it should come into being after the others, simultaneously with the end.

Clearly.

Then the one is younger than the others and the others older than the one.

That also is clear in my judgment.

Well, and must not a beginning or any other part of the one or of anything, if it be a part and not parts, being a part, be also of necessity one?

Certainly.

And will not the one come into being together with each part—together with the first part when that comes into being, and together with the second part and with all the rest, and will not be wanting to any part, which is added to any other part until it has reached the last and become one whole; it will be wanting neither to the middle, nor to the first, nor to the last, nor to any of them, while the process of becoming is going on?

True.

Then the one is of the same age with all the others, so that if the one itself does not contradict its own nature, it will be neither prior nor poste-
rior to the others, but simultaneous; and according to this argument the 154a
one will be neither older nor younger than the others, nor the others than the one, but according to the previous argument the one will be older and younger than the others and the others than the one.

Certainly.

After this manner then the one is and has become. But as to its becoming older and younger than the others, and the others than the one, and neither older nor younger, what shall we say? Shall we say as of being so also of becoming, or otherwise?

b I cannot answer.

But I can venture to say, that even if one thing were older or younger than another, it could not become older or younger in a greater degree than it was at first; for equals added to unequals, whether to periods of time or to anything else, leave the difference between them the same as at first.

Of course.

c Then that which is, cannot become older or younger than that which is, since the difference of age is always the same; the one is and has become older and the other younger; but they are no longer becoming so.

True.

And the one which is does not therefore become either older or younger than the others which are.

No.

But consider whether they may not become older and younger in another way.

In what way?

Just as the one was proven to be older than the others and the others than the one.

And what of that?

If the one is older than the others, has come into being a longer time than the others.

d Yes.

But consider again; if we add equal time to a greater and a less time, will the greater differ from the less time by an equal or by a smaller portion than before?

By a smaller portion.

Then the difference between the age of the one and the age of the others will not be afterwards so great as at first, but if an equal time be added to both of them they will differ less and less in age?

Yes.

And that which differs in age from some other less than formerly, from
e being older will become younger in relation to that other than which it
was older?

Yes, younger.

And if the one becomes younger the others aforesaid will become older than they were before, in relation to the one.

Certainly.

Then that which had become younger becomes older relatively to that
which previously had become and was older; it never really is older, but is
always becoming, for the one is always growing on the side of youth and the
other on the side of age. And in like manner the older is always in process
of becoming younger than the younger; for as they are always going in 155a
opposite directions they become in ways the opposite to one another, the
younger older than the older, and the older younger than the younger.
They cannot, however, have become; for if they had already become they
would be and not merely become. But that is impossible; for they are always
becoming both older and younger than one another: the one becomes
younger than the others because it was seen to be older and prior, and the
others become older than the one because they came into being later; and b
in the same way the others are in the same relation to the one, because they
were seen to be older, and prior to the one.

That is clear.

Inasmuch then, one thing does not become older or younger than
another, in that they always differ from each other by an equal number,
the one cannot become older or younger than the others, nor the others
than the one; but inasmuch as that which came into being earlier and that
which came into being later must continually differ from each other by a c
different portion—in this point of view the others must become older and
younger than the one, and the one than the others.

Certainly.

For all these reasons, then, the one is and becomes older and younger than itself and the others, and neither is nor becomes older or younger than itself or the others.

Certainly.

But since the one partakes of time, and partakes of becoming older and
younger, must it not also partake of the past, the present, and the future? d

Of course it must.

Then the one was and is and will be, and was becoming and is becoming and will become?

Certainly.

And there is and was and will be something which is in relation to it and belongs to it?

True.

And since we have at this moment opinion and knowledge and perception of the one, there is opinion and knowledge and perception of it?

Quite right.

Then there is name and expression for it, and it is named and
e expressed, and everything of this kind which appertains to other things appertains to the one.

Certainly, that is true.

Yet once more and for the third time, let us consider: If the one is both one and many, as we have described, and is neither one nor many, and participates in time, must it not, in as far as it is one, at times partake of being, and in as far as it is not one, at times not partake of being?

Certainly.

But can it partake of being when not partaking of being, or not partake of being when partaking of being?

Impossible.

Then the one partakes and does not partake of being at different times, for that is the only way in which it can partake and not partake of the same.

True.

156a And is there not also a time at which it assumes being and relinquishes being—for how can it have and not have the same thing unless it receives and also gives it up at some time?

Impossible.

And the assuming of being is what you would call becoming?

I should.

And the relinquishing of being you would call destruction?

I should.

The one then, as would appear, becomes and is destroyed by taking and giving up being.

Certainly.

And being one and many and in process of becoming and being
b destroyed, when it becomes one it ceases to be many, and when many, it ceases to be one?

Certainly.

And as it becomes one and many, must it not inevitably experience separation and aggregation?

Inevitably.

And whenever it becomes like and unlike it must be assimilated and dissimilated?

Yes.

And when it becomes greater or less or equal it must grow or diminish or be equalized?

True. c

And when being in motion it rests, and when being at rest it changes to motion, it can surely be in no time at all?

How can it?

But that a thing which is previously at rest should be afterwards in motion, or previously in motion and afterwards at rest, without experiencing change, is impossible.

Impossible.

And surely there cannot be a time in which a thing can be at once neither in motion nor at rest?

There cannot. d

But neither can it change without changing.

True.

When then does it change; for it cannot change either when at rest, or when in motion, or when in time?

It cannot.

And does this strange thing in which it is at the time of changing really exist?

What thing?

The moment. For the moment seems to imply a something out of
which change takes place into either of two states; for the change is not
from the state of rest as such, nor from the state of motion as such; but
there is this curious nature which we call the moment lying between rest e
and motion, not being in any time; and into this and out of this what is in
motion changes into rest, and what is at rest into motion.

So it appears.

And the one then, since it is at rest and also in motion, will change to either, for only in this way can it be in both. And in changing it changes in a moment, and when it is changing it will be in no time, and will not then be either in motion or at rest.

It will not.

And it will be in the same case in relation to the other changes, when
it passes from being into cessation of being, or from not-being into
becoming—then it passes between certain states of motion and rest, and 157a
neither is nor is not, nor becomes nor is destroyed.

Very true.

And on the same principle, in the passage from one to many and from
many to one, the one is neither one nor many, neither separated nor
b aggregated; and in the passage from like to unlike, and from unlike to
like, it is neither like nor unlike, neither in a state of assimilation nor of
dissimilation; and in the passage from small to great and equal and back
again, it will be neither small nor great, nor equal, nor in a state of increase,
or diminution, or equalization.

True.

All these, then, are the affections of the one, if the one has being.

Of course.

1.aa. But if one is, what will happen to the others—is not that also to be considered?

Yes.

Let us show then, if one is, what will be the affections of the others than the one.

Let us do so.

Inasmuch as there are things other than the one, the others are not the one; for if they were they could not be other than the one.

c Very true.

Nor are the others altogether without the one, but in a certain way they participate in the one.

In what way?

Because the others are other than the one inasmuch as they have parts; for if they had no parts they would be simply one.

Right.

And parts, as we affirm, have relation to a whole?

So we say.

And a whole must necessarily be one made up of many; and the parts will be parts of the one, for each of the parts is not a part of many, but of a whole.

How do you mean?

d If anything were a part of many, being itself one of them, it will surely
be a part of itself, which is impossible, and it will be a part of each one of
the other parts, if of all; for if not a part of some one, it will be a part
of all the others but this one, and thus will not be a part of each one; and
if not a part of each, one it will not be a part of any one of the many;
and not being a part of any one, it cannot be a part or anything else of all
those things of none of which it is anything.

Clearly not.

Then the part is not a part of the many, nor of all, but is of a certain single form, which we call a whole, being one perfect unity framed out of all—of this the part will be a part.

Certainly. e

If, then, the others have parts, they will participate in the whole and in the one.

True.

Then the others than the one must be one perfect whole, having parts.

Certainly.

And the same argument holds of each part, for the part must participate in the one; for if each of the parts is a part, this means, I suppose, that 158a
it is one separate from the rest and self-related; otherwise it is not each.

True.

But when we speak of the part participating in the one, it must clearly be other than one; for if not, it would not merely have participated, but would have been one; whereas only the itself can be one.

Very true.

Both the whole and the part must participate in the one; for the whole will be one whole, of which the parts will be parts; and each part will be one part of the whole which is the whole of the part.

True.

And will not the things which participate in the one, be other than it? b

Of course.

And the things which are other than the one will be many; for if the things which are other than the one were neither one nor more than one, they would be nothing.

True.

But, seeing that the things which participate in the one as a part, and
in the one as a whole, are more than one, must not those very things which
participate in the one be infinite in number? c

How so?

Let us look at the matter thus: Is it not a fact that in partaking of the one they are not one, and do not partake of the one at the very time when they are partaking of it?

Clearly.

They do so then as multitudes in which the one is not present?

Very true.

And if we were to abstract from them in idea the very smallest fraction, must not that least fraction, if it does not partake of the one, be a multitude and not one?

It must.

And if we continue to look at the other side of their nature, regarded simply, and in itself, will not they, as far as we see them, be unlimited in number?

Certainly.

And yet, when each several part becomes a part, then the parts have a
d limit in relation to the whole and to each other, and the whole in relation to the parts.

Just so.

The result to the others than the one is that the union of themselves and the one appears to create a new element in them which gives to them limitation in relation to one another; whereas in their own nature they have no limit.

That is clear.

Then the others than the one, both as whole and parts, are infinite, and also partake of limit.

Certainly.

e Then they are both like and unlike one another and themselves.

How is that?

Inasmuch as they are unlimited in their own nature, they are all affected in the same way.

True.

And inasmuch as they all partake of limit, they are all affected in the same way.

Of course.

But inasmuch as their state is both limited and unlimited, they are affected in opposite ways.

159a Yes.

And opposites are the most unlike of things.

Certainly.

Considered, then, in regard to either one of their affections, they will be like themselves and one another; considered in reference to both of them together, most opposed and most unlike.

That appears to be true.

Then the others are both like and unlike themselves and one another?

True.

And they are the same and also different from one another, and in motion and at rest, and experience every sort of opposite affection, as may be proved without difficulty of them, since they have been shown to have experienced the affections aforesaid?

True. b

1.bb. Suppose, now, that we leave the further discussion of these matters as evident, and consider again upon the hypothesis that the one is, whether opposite of all this is or is not equally true of the others.

By all means.

Then let us begin again, and ask, If one is, what must be the affections of the others?

Let us ask that question.

Must not the one be distinct from the others, and the others from the one?

Why so?

Why, because there is nothing else beside them which is distinct from c
both of them; for the expression "one and the others" includes all things.

Yes, all things.

Then we cannot suppose that there is anything different from them in which both the one and the others might exist?

There is nothing.

Then the one and the others are never in the same?

True.

Then they are separated from each other?

Yes.

And we surely cannot say that what is truly one has parts?

Impossible.

Then the one will not be in the others as a whole, nor as part, if it be separated from the others, and has no parts?

Impossible.

Then there is no way in which the others can partake of the one, if they do not partake either in whole or in part?

It would seem not.

Then there is no way in which the others are one, or have in them- d
selves any unity?

There is not.

Nor are the others many; for if they were many, each part of them would be a part of the whole; but now the others, not partaking in any way of the one, are neither one nor many, nor whole, nor part.

True.

Then the others neither are nor contain two or three, if entirely deprived of the one?

e True.

Then the others are neither like nor unlike the one, nor is likeness and unlikeness in them; for if they were like and unlike, or had in them likeness and unlikeness, they would have two natures in them opposite to one another.

That is clear.

But for that which partakes of nothing to partake of two things was held by us to be impossible?

Impossible.

Then the others are neither like nor unlike nor both, for if they were like or unlike they would partake of one of those two natures, which would be one thing, and if they were both they would partake of opposites which would be two things, and this has been shown to be impossible.

True.

Therefore they are neither the same, nor other, nor in motion, nor at
160a rest, nor in a state of becoming, nor of being destroyed, nor greater, nor less, nor equal, nor have they experienced anything else of the sort; for, if they are capable of experiencing any such affection, they will participate in one and two and three, and odd and even, and in these, as has
b been proved, they do not participate, seeing that they are altogether and in every way devoid of the one.

Very true.

Therefore if one is, the one is all things, and also nothing, both in relation to itself and to other things.

Certainly.

2.a. Well, and ought we not to consider next what will be the consequence if the one is not?

Yes; we ought.

What is the meaning of the hypothesis—If the one is not; is there any difference between this and the hypothesis—If the not one is not?

There is a difference, certainly.

Is there a difference only, or rather are not the two expressions—if
c the one is not, and if the not one is not, entirely opposed?

They are entirely opposed.

And suppose a person to say: If greatness is not, if smallness is not, or anything of that sort, does he not mean, whenever he uses such an expression, that "what is not" is other than other things?

To be sure.

And so when he says "If one is not" he clearly means, that what "is not" is other than all others; we know what he means—do we not?

Yes, we do.

When he says "one," he says something which is known; and secondly something which is other than all other things; it makes no difference
whether he predicate of one being or not-being, for that which is said "not d
to be" is known to be something all the same, and is distinguished from other things.

Certainly.

Then I will begin again, and ask: If one is not, what are the consequences? In the first place, as would appear, there is a knowledge of it, or the very meaning of the words, "if one is not," would not be known.

True.

Secondly, the others differ from it, or it could not be described as different from the others?

Certainly.

Difference, then, belongs to it as well as knowledge; for in speaking
of the one as different from the others, we do not speak of a difference in e
the others, but in the one.

Clearly so.

Moreover, the one that is not is something and partakes of relation to "that," and "this," and "these," and the like, and is an attribute of "this"; for the one, or the others than the one, could not have been spoken of, nor could any attribute or relative of the one that is not have been or been spoken of, nor could it have been said to be anything, if it did not partake of "some," or of the other relations just now mentioned.

True.

Being, then, cannot be ascribed to the one, since it is not; but the one
that is not may or rather must participate in many things, if it and noth- 161a
ing else is not; if, however, neither the one nor the one that is not is supposed not to be, and we are speaking of something of a different nature, we can predicate nothing of it. But supposing that the one that is not and nothing else is not, then it must participate in the predicate "that," and in many others.

Certainly.

And it will have unlikeness in relation to the others, for the others being different from the one will be of a different kind.

Certainly.

b And are not things of a different kind also other in kind?

Of course.

And are not things other in kind unlike?

They are unlike.

And if they are unlike the one, that which they are unlike will clearly be unlike them?

Clearly so.

Then the one will have unlikeness in respect of which the others are unlike it?

That would seem to be true.

And if unlikeness to other things is attributed to it, it must have likeness to itself.

How so?

If the one have unlikeness to one, something else must be meant; nor will the hypothesis relate to one; but it will relate to something other than one?

Quite so.

c But that cannot be.

No.

Then the one must have likeness to itself?

It must.

Again, it is not equal to the others; for if it were equal, then it would at once be and be like them in virtue of the equality; but if one has no being, then it can neither be nor be like?

It cannot.

But since it is not equal to the others, neither can the others be equal to it?

Certainly not.

And things that are not equal are unequal?

True.

And they are unequal to an unequal?

Of course.

Then the one partakes of inequality, and in respect of this the others are unequal to it?

d Very true.

And inequality implies greatness and smallness?

Yes.

Then the one, if of such a nature, has greatness and smallness?

That appears to be true.

And greatness and smallness always stand apart?

True.

Then there is always something between them?

There is.

And can you think of anything else which is between them other than equality?

No, it is equality which lies between them.

Then that which has greatness and smallness also has equality, which lies between them?

That is clear. e

Then the one, which is not, partakes, as would appear, of greatness and smallness and equality?

Clearly.

Further, it must surely in a sort partake of being?

How so?

It must be so, for if not, then we should not speak the truth in saying that the one is not. But if we speak the truth, clearly we must say what is. Am I not right?

Yes.

And since we affirm that we speak truly, we must also affirm that we say what is?

Certainly. 162a

Then, as would appear, the one, when it is not, is; for if it were not to be when it is not, but (Or, "to remit something of existence in relation to not-being.") were to relinquish something of being, so as to become not-being, it would at once be.

Quite true.

Then the one which is not, if it is to maintain itself, must have the being of not-being as the bond of not-being, just as being must have as a bond the not-being of not-being in order to perfect its own being; for the truest assertion of the being of being and of the not-being of not-being
is when being partakes of the being of being, and not of the being of b
not-being—that is, the perfection of being; and when not-being does not partake of the not-being of not-being but of the being of not-being—that is the perfection of not-being.

Most true.

Since then what is partakes of not-being, and what is not of being, must not the one also partake of being in order not to be?

Certainly.

Then the one, if it is not, clearly has being?

Clearly.

And has not-being also, if it is not?

Of course.

But can anything which is in a certain state not be in that state without changing?

Impossible.

c Then everything which is and is not in a certain state, implies change?

Certainly.

And change is motion—we may say that?

Yes, motion.

And the one has been proved both to be and not to be?

Yes.

And therefore is and is not in the same state?

Yes.

Thus the one that is not has been shown to have motion also, because it changes from being to not-being?

That appears to be true.

But surely if it is nowhere among what is, as is the fact, since it is not, it cannot change from one place to another?

Impossible.

Then it cannot move by changing place?

d No.

Nor can it turn on the same spot, for it nowhere touches the same, for the same is, and that which is not cannot be reckoned among things that are?

It cannot.

Then the one, if it is not, cannot turn in that in which it is not?

No.

Neither can the one, whether it is or is not, be altered into other than itself, for if it altered and became different from itself, then we could not be still speaking of the one, but of something else?

True.

But if the one neither suffers alteration, nor turns round in the same place, nor changes place, can it still be capable of motion?

Impossible.

Now that which is unmoved must surely be at rest, and that which is at e
rest must stand still?

Certainly.

Then the one that is not, stands still, and is also in motion?

That seems to be true.

But if it be in motion it must necessarily undergo alteration, for anything which is moved, insofar as it is moved, is no longer in the same state, 163a
but in another?

Yes.

Then the one, being moved, is altered?

Yes.

And, further, if not moved in any way, it will not be altered in any way?

No.

Then, insofar as the one that is not is moved, it is altered, but insofar as it is not moved, it is not altered?

Right.

Then the one that is not is altered and is not altered?

That is clear.

And must not that which is altered become other than it previously b
was, and lose its former state and be destroyed; but that which is not altered can neither come into being nor be destroyed?

Very true.

And the one that is not, being altered, becomes and is destroyed; and not being altered, neither becomes nor is destroyed; and so the one that is not becomes and is destroyed, and neither becomes nor is destroyed?

True.

2.b. And now, let us go back once more to the beginning, and see whether these or some other consequences will follow.

Let us do as you say.

If one is not, we ask what will happen in respect of one? That is c
the question.

Yes.

Do not the words "is not" signify absence of being in that to which we apply them?

Just so.

And when we say that a thing is not, do we mean that it is not in one way but is in another? or do we mean, absolutely, that what is not has in no sort or way or kind participation of being?

Quite absolutely.

Then, that which is not cannot be, or in any way participate in being?

d It cannot.

And did we not mean by becoming, and being destroyed, the assumption of being and the loss of being?

Nothing else.

And can that which has no participation in being, either assume or lose being?

Impossible.

The one then, since it in no way is, cannot have or lose or assume being in any way?

True.

e Then the one that is not, since it in no way partakes of being, neither perishes nor becomes?

No.

Then it is not altered at all; for if it were it would become and be destroyed?

True.

But if it be not altered it cannot be moved?

Certainly not.

Nor can we say that it stands, if it is nowhere; for that which stands must always be in one and the same spot?

Of course.

Then we must say that the one which is not never stands still and never moves?

Neither.

Nor is there any existing thing which can be attributed to it; for if there had been, it would partake of being?

164a That is clear.

And therefore neither smallness, nor greatness, nor equality, can be attributed to it?

No.

Nor yet likeness nor difference, either in relation to itself or to others?

Clearly not.

Well, and if nothing should be attributed to it, can other things be attributed to it?

Certainly not.

And therefore other things can neither be like or unlike, the same, or different in relation to it?

They cannot.

Nor can what is not, be anything, or be this thing, or be related to or the attribute of this or that or other, or be past, present, or future. Nor can
knowledge, or opinion, or perception, or expression, or name, or any b
other thing that is, have any concern with it?

No.

Then the one that is not has no condition of any kind?

Such appears to be the conclusion.

2.aa. Yet once more; if one is not, what becomes of the others? Let us determine that.

Yes; let us determine that.

The others must surely be; for if they, like the one, were not, we could not be now speaking of them.

True.

But to speak of the others implies difference—the terms "other" and c
"different" are synonymous?

True.

Other means other than other, and different, different from the different?

Yes.

Then, if there are to be others, there is something than which they will be other?

Certainly.

And what can that be? For if the one is not, they will not be other than the one.

They will not.

Then they will be other than each other; for the only remaining alternative is that they are other than nothing.

True.

And they are each other than one another, as being plural and not
singular; for if one is not, they cannot be singular, but every particle of d
them is infinite in number; and even if a person takes that which appears to be the smallest fraction, this, which seemed one, in a moment evanesces into many, as in a dream, and from being the smallest becomes very great, in comparison with the fractions into which it is split up?

Very true.

And in such particles the others will be other than one another, if others are, and the one is not?

Exactly.

And will there not be many particles, each appearing to be one, but not being one, if one is not?

e True.

And it would seem that number can be predicated of them if each of them appears to be one, though it is really many?

It can.

And there will seem to be odd and even among them, which will also have no reality, if one is not?

Yes.

And there will appear to be a least among them; and even this will seem large and manifold in comparison with the many small fractions which are contained in it?

165a Certainly.

And each particle will be imagined to be equal to the many and little; for it could not have appeared to pass from the greater to the less without having appeared to arrive at the middle; and thus would arise the appearance of equality.

Yes.

And having neither beginning, middle, nor end, each separate particle yet appears to have a limit in relation to itself and other.

How so?

Because, when a person conceives of any one of these as such, prior
b to the beginning another beginning appears, and there is another end, remaining after the end, and in the middle truer middles within but smaller, because no unity can be conceived of any of them, since the one is not.

Very true.

And so all being, whatever we think of, must be broken up into fractions, for a particle will have to be conceived of without unity?

Certainly.

c And such being when seen indistinctly and at a distance, appears to be one; but when seen near and with keen intellect, every single thing appears to be infinite, since it is deprived of the one, which is not?

Nothing more certain.

Then each of the others must appear to be infinite and finite, and one and many, if others than the one exist and not the one.

They must.

Then will they not appear to be like and unlike?

In what way?

Just as in a picture things appear to be all one to a person standing at a distance, and to be in the same state and alike?

True.

But when you approach them, they appear to be many and different; d
and because of the appearance of the difference, different in kind from, and unlike, themselves?

True.

And so must the particles appear to be like and unlike themselves and each other.

Certainly.

And must they not be the same and yet different from one another, and in contact with themselves, although they are separated, and having every sort of motion, and every sort of rest, and becoming and being destroyed, and in neither state, and the like, all which things may be easily enumerated, if the one is not and the many are?

Most true. e

2.bb. Once more, let us go back to the beginning, and ask if the one is not, and the others of the one are, what will follow.

Let us ask that question.

In the first place, the others will not be one?

Impossible.

Nor will they be many; for if they were many one would be contained in them. But if no one of them is one, all of them are nought, and therefore they will not be many.

True.

If there be no one in the others, the others are neither many nor one.

They are not.

Nor do they appear either as one or many. 166a

Why not?

Because the others have no sort or manner or way of communion with any sort of not-being, nor can anything which is not, be connected with any of the others; for that which is not has no parts.

True.

Nor is there an opinion or any appearance of not-being in connection with the others, nor is not-being ever in any way attributed to the others.

No.

Then if one is not, there is no conception of any of the others either as one or many; for you cannot conceive the many without the one. b

You cannot.

Then if one is not, the others neither are, nor can be conceived to be either one or many?

It would seem not.

Nor as like or unlike?

No.

Nor as the same or different, nor in contact or separation, nor in any of those states which we enumerated as appearing to be; the others neither are nor appear to be any of these, if one is not?

True.

c Then may we not sum up the argument in a word and say truly: If one is not, then nothing is?

Certainly.

Let thus much be said; and further let us affirm what seems to be the truth, that, whether one is or is not, one and the others in relation to themselves and one another, all of them, in every way, are and are not, and appear to be and appear not to be.

Most true.

Theaetetus

Theaetetus

Persons of the Dialogue: Socrates, Theodorus, Theaetetus. Euclid and Terpsion meet in front of Euclid's house in Megara; they enter the house, and the dialogue is read to them by a servant.

Euclid: Have you only just arrived from the country, Terpsion? 142a

Terpsion: No, I came some time ago: and I have been in the Agora looking for you, and wondering that I could not find you.

Euclid: But I was not in the city.

Terpsion: Where then?

Euclid: As I was going down to the harbor, I met Theaetetus—he was being carried up to Athens from the army at Corinth.

Terpsion: Was he alive or dead?

Euclid: He was scarcely alive, for he has been badly wounded; but he b
was suffering even more from the sickness which has broken out in the army.

Terpsion: The dysentery, you mean?

Euclid: Yes.

Terpsion: Alas! What a loss he will be!

Euclid: Yes, Terpsion, he is a noble fellow; only today I heard some people highly praising his behavior in this very battle.

Terpsion: No wonder; I should rather be surprised at hearing anything else
of him. But why did he go on, instead of stopping at Megara? c

Euclid: He wanted to get home: although I entreated and advised him to remain, he would not listen to me; so I set him on his way, and turned

d back, and then I remembered what Socrates had said of him, and
thought how remarkably this, like all his predictions, had been fulfilled. I believe that he had seen him a little before his own death,
when Theaetetus was a youth, and he had a memorable conversation
with him, which he repeated to me when I came to Athens; he was full
of admiration of his genius, and said that he would most certainly be
a great man, if he lived.

TERPSION: The prophecy has certainly been fulfilled; but what was the conversation? Can you tell me?

EUCLID: No, indeed, not offhand; but I took notes of it as soon as I got
143a home; these I filled up from memory, writing them out at leisure; and
whenever I went to Athens, I asked Socrates about any point which I
had forgotten, and on my return I made corrections; thus I have nearly
the whole conversation written down.

TERPSION: I remember—you told me; and I have always been intending to ask you to show me the writing, but have put off doing so; and now, why should we not read it through? Having just come from the country, I should greatly like to rest.

b *EUCLID*: I too shall be very glad of a rest, for I went with Theaetetus as far
as Erineum. Let us go in, then, and, while we are reposing, the servant
shall read to us.

TERPSION: Very good.

EUCLID: Here is the roll, Terpsion; I may observe that I have introduced
Socrates, not as narrating to me, but as actually conversing with the
c persons whom he mentioned—these were, Theodorus the geometrician (of Cyrene), and Theaetetus. I have omitted, for the sake of
convenience, the interlocutory words "I said," "I remarked," which he
used when he spoke of himself, and again, "he agreed," or "disagreed,"
in the answer, lest the repetition of them should be troublesome.

TERPSION: Quite right, Euclid.

EUCLID: And now, boy, you may take the roll and read.

EUCLID'S SERVANT READS.

SOCRATES: If I cared enough about the Cyrenians, Theodorus, I would ask
d you whether there are any rising geometricians or philosophers in that
part of the world. But I am more interested in our own Athenian youth,
and I would rather know who among them are likely to do well. I
observe them as far as I can myself, and I enquire of anyone whom they
follow, and I see that a great many of them follow you, in which they are

quite right, considering your eminence in geometry and in other ways. e
Tell me then, if you have met with anyone who is good for anything.

THEODORUS: Yes, Socrates, I have become acquainted with one very remarkable Athenian youth, whom I commend to you as well worthy of your
attention. If he had been a beauty I should have been afraid to praise
him, lest you should suppose that I was in love with him; but he is no
beauty, and you must not be offended if I say that he is very like you; for
he has a snub nose and projecting eyes, although these features are less 144a
marked in him than in you. Seeing, then, that he has no personal attrac-
tions, I may freely say, that in all my acquaintance, which is very large, I
never knew anyone who was his equal in natural gifts: for he has a quickness of apprehension which is almost unrivalled, and he is exceedingly
gentle, and also the most courageous of men; there is a union of qualities
in him such as I have never seen in any other, and should scarcely have
thought possible; for those who, like him, have quick and ready and
retentive wits, have generally also quick tempers; they are ships without
ballast, and go darting about, and are mad rather than courageous; and b
the steadier sort, when they have to face study, prove stupid and cannot
remember. Whereas he moves surely and smoothly and successfully in
the path of knowledge and enquiry; and he is full of gentleness, flowing
on silently like a river of oil; at his age, it is wonderful.

SOCRATES: That is good news; whose son is he?

THEODORUS: The name of his father I have forgotten, but the youth himself
is the middle one of those who are approaching us; he and his com- c
panions have been anointing themselves in the outer court, and now
they seem to have finished, and are coming towards us. Look and see
whether you know him.

SOCRATES: I know the youth, but I do not know his name; he is the son of Euphronius the Sunian, who was himself an eminent man, and such another as his son is, according to your account of him; I believe that he left a considerable fortune.

THEODORUS: Theaetetus, Socrates, is his name; but I rather think that the d
property disappeared in the hands of trustees; notwithstanding which
he is wonderfully liberal.

SOCRATES: He must be a fine fellow; tell him to come and sit by me.

THEODORUS: I will. Come hither, Theaetetus, and sit by Socrates.

SOCRATES: By all means, Theaetetus, in order that I may see the reflection
of myself in your face, for Theodorus says that we are alike; and yet if e

each of us held in his hands a lyre, and he said that they were tuned alike, should we at once take his word, or should we ask whether he who said so was or was not a musician?

THEAETETUS: We should ask.

SOCRATES: And if we found that he was, we should take his word; and if not, not?

THEAETETUS: True.

SOCRATES: And if this supposed likeness of our faces is a matter of any inter-
145a est to us, we should enquire whether he who says that we are alike is a painter or not?

THEAETETUS: Certainly we should.

SOCRATES: And is Theodorus a painter?

THEAETETUS: I never heard that he was.

SOCRATES: Is he a geometrician?

THEAETETUS: Of course he is, Socrates.

SOCRATES: And is he an astronomer and calculator and musician, and in general an educated man?

THEAETETUS: I think so.

SOCRATES: If, then, he remarks on a similarity in our persons, either by way of praise or blame, there is no particular reason why we should attend to him.

THEAETETUS: I should say not.

b *SOCRATES*: But if he praises the virtue or wisdom which are the mental endowments of either of us, then he who hears the praises will naturally desire to examine him who is praised: and he again should be willing to exhibit himself.

THEAETETUS: Very true, Socrates.

SOCRATES: Then now is the time, my dear Theaetetus, for me to examine, and for you to exhibit; since although Theodorus has praised many a citizen and stranger in my hearing, never did I hear him praise anyone as he has been praising you.

c *THEAETETUS*: I am glad to hear it, Socrates; but what if he was only in jest?

SOCRATES: Nay, Theodorus is not given to jesting; and I cannot allow you to retract your consent on any such pretence as that. If you do, he will have to swear to his words; and we are perfectly sure that no one will be found to impugn him. Do not be shy then, but stand to your word.

THEAETETUS: I suppose I must, if you wish it.

SOCRATES: In the first place, I should like to ask what you learn of Theodorus: something of geometry, perhaps?

THEAETETUS: Yes.

SOCRATES: And astronomy and harmony and calculation? d

THEAETETUS: I do my best.

SOCRATES: Yes, my boy, and so do I; and my desire is to learn of him, or of anybody who seems to understand these things. And I get on pretty well in general; but there is a little difficulty which I want you and the company to aid me in investigating. Will you answer me a question: "Is not learning growing wiser about that which you learn?"

THEAETETUS: Of course.

SOCRATES: And by wisdom the wise are wise?

THEAETETUS: Yes.

SOCRATES: And is that different in any way from knowledge? e

THEAETETUS: What?

SOCRATES: Wisdom; are not men wise in that which they know?

THEAETETUS: Certainly they are.

SOCRATES: Then wisdom and knowledge are the same?

THEAETETUS: Yes.

SOCRATES: Herein lies the difficulty which I can never solve to my
satisfaction—What is knowledge? Can we answer that question? What 146a
say you? Which of us will speak first? Whoever misses shall sit down, as at a game of ball, and shall be donkey, as the boys say; he who lasts out his competitors in the game without missing, shall be our king, and shall have the right of putting to us any questions which he pleases. . . . Why is there no reply? I hope, Theodorus, that I am not betrayed into rudeness by my love of conversation? I only want to make us talk and be friendly and sociable.

THEODORUS: The reverse of rudeness, Socrates: but I would rather that b
you would ask one of the young fellows; for the truth is, that I am unused to your game of question and answer, and I am too old to learn; the young will be more suitable, and they will improve more than I shall, for youth is always able to improve. And so having made a beginning with Theaetetus, I would advise you to go on with him and not let him off.

SOCRATES: Do you hear, Theaetetus, what Theodorus says? The philosopher, whom you would not like to disobey, and whose word ought to c
be a command to a young man, bids me interrogate you. Take courage, then, and nobly say what you think that knowledge is.

THEAETETUS: Well, Socrates, I will answer as you and he bid me; and if I make a mistake, you will doubtless correct me.

Socrates: We will, if we can.

Theaetetus: Then, I think that the sciences which I learn from Theodorus—
d geometry, and those which you just now mentioned—are knowledge; and I would include the art of the cobbler and other craftsmen; these, each and all of, them, are knowledge.

Socrates: Too much, Theaetetus, too much; the nobility and liberality of your nature make you give many and diverse things, when I am asking for one simple thing.

Theaetetus: What do you mean, Socrates?

Socrates: Perhaps nothing. I will endeavor, however, to explain what I believe to be my meaning: When you speak of cobbling, you mean the art or science of making shoes?

Theaetetus: Just so.

e *Socrates*: And when you speak of carpentering, you mean the art of making wooden implements?

Theaetetus: I do.

Socrates: In both cases you define the subject matter of each of the two arts?

Theaetetus: True.

Socrates: But that, Theaetetus, was not the point of my question: we wanted to know not the subjects, nor yet the number of the arts or sciences, for we were not going to count them, but we wanted to know the nature of knowledge in the abstract. Am I not right?

Theaetetus: Perfectly right.

147a *Socrates*: Let me offer an illustration: Suppose that a person were to ask about some very trivial and obvious thing—for example, What is clay? And we were to reply, that there is a clay of potters, there is a clay of oven- makers, there is a clay of brick-makers; would not the answer be ridiculous?

Theaetetus: Truly.

Socrates: In the first place, there would be an absurdity in assuming that he who asked the question would understand from our answer the
b nature of "clay," merely because we added "of the image-makers," or of any other workers. How can a man understand the name of anything, when he does not know the nature of it?

Theaetetus: He cannot.

Socrates: Then he who does not know what science or knowledge is, has no knowledge of the art or science of making shoes?

Theaetetus: None.

Socrates: Nor of any other science?

Theaetetus: No.

Socrates: And when a man is asked what science or knowledge is, to give in
answer the name of some art or science is ridiculous; for the question c
is, "What is knowledge?" and he replies, "A knowledge of this or that."

Theaetetus: True.

Socrates: Moreover, he might answer shortly and simply, but he makes an enormous circuit. For example, when asked about the clay, he might have said simply, that clay is moistened earth—what sort of clay is not to the point.

Theaetetus: Yes, Socrates, there is no difficulty as you put the question. You
mean, if I am not mistaken, something like what occurred to me and to d
my friend here, your namesake Socrates, in a recent discussion.

Socrates: What was that, Theaetetus?

Theaetetus: Theodorus was writing out for us something about roots, such
as the roots of three or five, showing that they are incommensurable
by the unit: he selected other examples up to seventeen—there he
stopped. Now as there are innumerable roots, the notion occurred to e
us of attempting to include them all under one name or class.

Socrates: And did you find such a class?

Theaetetus: I think that we did; but I should like to have your opinion.

Socrates: Let me hear.

Theaetetus: We divided all numbers into two classes: those which are made up of equal factors multiplying into one another, which we compared to square figures and called square or equilateral numbers; that was one class.

Socrates: Very good.

Theaetetus: The intermediate numbers, such as three and five, and every
other number which is made up of unequal factors, either of a greater 148a
multiplied by a less, or of a less multiplied by a greater, and when
regarded as a figure, is contained in unequal sides; all these we compared to oblong figures, and called them oblong numbers.

Socrates: Capital; and what followed?

Theaetetus: The lines, or sides, which have for their squares the equilateral plane numbers, were called by us lengths or magnitudes; and
the lines which are the roots of (or whose squares are equal to) the
oblong numbers, were called powers or roots; the reason of this latter b
name being, that they are commensurable with the former [i.e., with
the so-called lengths or magnitudes] not in linear measurement, but
in the value of the superficial content of their squares; and the same
about solids.

Socrates: Excellent, my boys; I think that you fully justify the praises of Theodorus, and that he will not be found guilty of false witness.

Theaetetus: But I am unable, Socrates, to give you a similar answer about knowledge, which is what you appear to want; and therefore Theodorus is a deceiver after all.

c *Socrates*: Well, but if someone were to praise you for running, and to say that he never met your equal among boys, and afterwards you were beaten in a race by a grown-up man, who was a great runner—would the praise be any the less true?

Theaetetus: Certainly not.

Socrates: And is the discovery of the nature of knowledge so small a matter, as just now said? Is it not one which would task the powers of men perfect in every way?

Theaetetus: By heaven, they should be the top of all perfection!

Socrates: Well, then, be of good cheer; do not say that Theodorus was
d mistaken about you, but do your best to ascertain the true nature of knowledge, as well as of other things.

Theaetetus: I am eager enough, Socrates, if that would bring to light the truth.

Socrates: Come, you made a good beginning just now; let your own answer about roots be your model, and as you comprehended them all in one class, try and bring the many sorts of knowledge under one definition.

e *Theaetetus*: I can assure you, Socrates, that I have tried very often, when the report of questions asked by you was brought to me; but I can neither persuade myself that I have a satisfactory answer to give, nor hear of anyone who answers as you would have him; and I cannot shake off a feeling of anxiety.

Socrates: These are the pangs of labor, my dear Theaetetus; you have something within you which you are bringing to the birth.

Theaetetus: I do not know, Socrates; I only say what I feel.

149a *Socrates*: And have you never heard, simpleton, that I am the son of a midwife, brave and burly, whose name was Phaenarete?

Theaetetus: Yes, I have.

Socrates: And that I myself practice midwifery?

Theaetetus: No, never.

Socrates: Let me tell you that I do though, my friend: but you must not reveal the secret, as the world in general have not found me out; and therefore they only say of me, that I am the strangest of mortals and drive men to their wits' end. Did you ever hear that too?

Theaetetus: Yes. b

Socrates: Shall I tell you the reason?

Theaetetus: By all means.

Socrates: Bear in mind the whole business of the midwives, and then you will see my meaning better: No woman, as you are probably aware, who is still able to conceive and bear, attends other women, but only those who are past bearing.

Theaetetus: Yes, I know.

Socrates: The reason of this is said to be that Artemis—the goddess of
childbirth—is not a mother, and she honors those who are like herself; c
but she could not allow the barren to be midwives, because human nature cannot know the mystery of an art without experience; and therefore she assigned this office to those who are too old to bear.

Theaetetus: I dare say.

Socrates: And I dare say too, or rather I am absolutely certain, that the midwives know better than others who is pregnant and who is not?

Theaetetus: Very true.

Socrates: And by the use of potions and incantations they are able to
arouse the pangs and to soothe them at will; they can make those bear d
who have a difficulty in bearing, and if they think fit they can smother the embryo in the womb.

Theaetetus: They can.

Socrates: Did you ever remark that they are also most cunning matchmakers, and have a thorough knowledge of what unions are likely to produce a brave brood?

Theaetetus: No, never.

Socrates: Then let me tell you that this is their greatest pride, more than cut-
ting the umbilical cord. And if you reflect, you will see that the same art e
which cultivates and gathers in the fruits of the earth, will be most likely to know in what soils the several plants or seeds should be deposited.

Theaetetus: Yes, the same art.

Socrates: And do you suppose that with women the case is otherwise?

Theaetetus: I should think not.

Socrates: Certainly not; but midwives are respectable women who have 150a
a character to lose, and they avoid this department of their profession, because they are afraid of being called procuresses, which is a name given to those who join together man and woman in an unlawful and unscientific way; and yet the true midwife is also the true and only matchmaker.

THEAETETUS: Clearly.

SOCRATES: Such are the midwives, whose task is a very important one, but
b not so important as mine; for women do not bring into the world at
one time real children, and at another time counterfeits which are
with difficulty distinguished from them; if they did, then the discern-
ment of the true and false birth would be the crowning achievement
of the art of midwifery—you would think so?

THEAETETUS: Indeed I should.

SOCRATES: Well, my art of midwifery is in most respects like theirs; but differs, in that I attend men and not women; and look after their souls
c when they are in labor, and not after their bodies: and the triumph of
my art is in thoroughly examining whether the thought which the
mind of the young man brings forth is a false idol or a noble and true
birth. And like the midwives, I am barren, and the reproach which is
often made against me, that I ask questions of others and have not the
wit to answer them myself, is very just—the reason is, that the god
compels me to be a midwife, but does not allow me to bring forth.
And therefore I am not myself at all wise, nor have I anything to show
which is the invention or birth of my own soul, but those who con-
d verse with me profit. Some of them appear dull enough at first, but
afterwards, as our acquaintance ripens, if the god is gracious to them,
they all make astonishing progress; and this in the opinion of others
as well as in their own. It is quite clear that they never learned anything
from me; the many fine discoveries to which they cling are of their
own making. But to me and the god they owe their delivery. And the
e proof of my words is, that many of them in their ignorance, either
in their self-conceit despising me, or falling under the influence of
others, have gone away too soon; and have not only lost the children
of whom I had previously delivered them by an ill bringing up, but
have stifled whatever else they had in them by evil communications,
being fonder of lies and shams than of the truth; and they have at last
ended by seeing themselves, as others see them, to be great fools. Aris-
51a teides, the son of Lysimachus, is one of them, and there are many
others. The truants often return to me, and beg that I would consort
with them again—they are ready to go to me on their knees—and
then, if my familiar allows, which is not always the case, I receive them,
and they begin to grow again. Dire are the pangs which my art is able
to arouse and to allay in those who consort with me, just like the
pangs of women in childbirth; night and day they are full of perplexity

and travail which is even worse than that of the women. So much for
them. And there are others, Theaetetus, who come to me apparently b
having nothing in them; and as I know that they have no need of my
art, I coax them into marrying someone, and by the grace of God I
can generally tell who is likely to do them good. Many of them I have
given away to Prodicus, and many to other inspired sages. I tell you this
long story, friend Theaetetus, because I suspect, as indeed you seem to
think yourself, that you are in labor—great with some conception.
Come then to me, who am a midwife's son and myself a midwife, and c
do your best to answer the questions which I will ask you. And if I
abstract and expose your firstborn, because I discover upon inspec-
tion that the conception which you have formed is a vain shadow, do
not quarrel with me on that account, as the manner of women is when
their first children are taken from them. For I have actually known
some who were ready to bite me when I deprived them of a darling
folly; they did not perceive that I acted from goodwill, not knowing
that no god is the enemy of man—that was not within the range of
their ideas; neither am I their enemy in all this, but it would be wrong
for me to admit falsehood, or to stifle the truth. Once more, then, d
Theaetetus, I repeat my old question, "What is knowledge?" and do
not say that you cannot tell; but quit yourself like a man, and by the
help of God you will be able to tell.

THEAETETUS: At any rate, Socrates, after such an exhortation I should be
ashamed of not trying to do my best. Now he who knows perceives what e
he knows, and, as far as I can see at present, knowledge is perception.

SOCRATES: Bravely said, boy; that is the way in which you should express your opinion. And now, let us examine together this conception of yours, and see whether it is a true birth or a mere wind-egg: You say that knowledge is perception?

THEAETETUS: Yes.

SOCRATES: Well, you have delivered yourself of a very important doctrine
about knowledge; it is indeed the opinion of Protagoras, who has 152a
another way of expressing it. Man, he says, is the measure of all things,
of the existence of things that are, and of the nonexistence of things
that are not: You have read him?

THEAETETUS: O yes, again and again.

SOCRATES: Does he not say that things are to you such as they appear to you, and to me such as they appear to me, and that you and I are men?

THEAETETUS: Yes, he says so.

b *Socrates*: A wise man is not likely to talk nonsense. Let us try to understand him: the same wind is blowing, and yet one of us may be cold and the other not, or one may be slightly and the other very cold?

Theaetetus: Quite true.

Socrates: Now is the wind, regarded not in relation to us but absolutely, cold or not; or are we to say, with Protagoras, that the wind is cold to him who is cold, and not to him who is not?

Theaetetus: I suppose the last.

Socrates: Then it must appear so to each of them?

Theaetetus: Yes.

Socrates: And "appears to him" means the same as "he perceives."

Theaetetus: True.

c *Socrates*: Then appearing and perceiving coincide in the case of hot and cold, and in similar instances; for things appear, or may be supposed to be, to each one such as he perceives them?

Theaetetus: Yes.

Socrates: Then perception is always of existence, and being the same as knowledge is unerring?

Theaetetus: Clearly.

Socrates: In the name of the Graces, what an almighty wise man Protagoras must have been! He spoke these things in a parable to the common herd, like you and me, but told the truth, "his Truth," (In allusion to a book of Protagoras' which bore this title.) in secret to his own disciples.

d *Theaetetus*: What do you mean, Socrates?

Socrates: I am about to speak of a high argument, in which all things are said
to be relative; you cannot rightly call anything by any name, such as great
or small, heavy or light, for the great will be small and the heavy light—
there is no single thing or quality, but out of motion and change and
admixture all things are becoming relatively to one another, which
e "becoming" is by us incorrectly called being, but is really becoming, for
nothing ever is, but all things are becoming. Summon all philosophers—
Protagoras, Heracleitus, Empedocles, and the rest of them, one after
another, and with the exception of Parmenides they will agree with you
in this. Summon the great masters of either kind of poetry—Epicharmus,
the prince of Comedy, and Homer of Tragedy; when the latter sings of

> Ocean whence sprang the gods, and mother Tethys,

does he not mean that all things are the offspring, of flux and motion?

Theaetetus: I think so.

Socrates: And who could take up arms against such a great army having 153a
Homer for its general, and not appear ridiculous? (Compare Cratylus.)

Theaetetus: Who indeed, Socrates?

Socrates: Yes, Theaetetus; and there are plenty of other proofs which will show that motion is the source of what is called being and becoming, and inactivity of not-being and destruction; for fire and warmth, which are supposed to be the parent and guardian of all other things, are born of movement and of friction, which is a kind of motion; is not this the origin of fire?

Theaetetus: It is. b

Socrates: And the race of animals is generated in the same way?

Theaetetus: Certainly.

Socrates: And is not the bodily habit spoiled by rest and idleness, but preserved for a long time by motion and exercise?

Theaetetus: True.

Socrates: And what of the mental habit? Is not the soul informed, and
improved, and preserved by study and attention, which are motions;
but when at rest, which in the soul only means want of attention and
study, is uninformed, and speedily forgets whatever she has learned? c

Theaetetus: True.

Socrates: Then motion is a good, and rest an evil, to the soul as well as to the body?

Theaetetus: Clearly.

Socrates: I may add, that breathless calm, stillness and the like waste and
impair, while wind and storm preserve; and the palmary argument of
all, which I strongly urge, is the golden chain in Homer, by which he
means the sun, thereby indicating that so long as the sun and the d
heavens go round in their orbits, all things human and divine are and
are preserved, but if they were chained up and their motions ceased,
then all things would be destroyed, and, as the saying is, turned
upside down.

Theaetetus: I believe, Socrates, that you have truly explained his meaning.

Socrates: Then now apply his doctrine to perception, my good friend, and
first of all to vision; that which you call white color is not in your eyes,
and is not a distinct thing which exists out of them. And you must not e
assign any place to it: for if it had position it would be, and be at rest,
and there would be no process of becoming.

Theaetetus: Then what is color?

SOCRATES: Let us carry the principle which has just been affirmed, that nothing is self-existent, and then we shall see that white, black, and
154a every other color, arises out of the eye meeting the appropriate motion, and that what we call a color is in each case neither the active nor the passive element, but something which passes between them, and is peculiar to each percipient; are you quite certain that the several colors appear to a dog or to any animal whatever as they appear to you?

THEAETETUS: Far from it.

SOCRATES: Or that anything appears the same to you as to another man? Are you so profoundly convinced of this? Rather would it not be true that it never appears exactly the same to you, because you are never exactly the same?

THEAETETUS: The latter.

b *SOCRATES*: And if that with which I compare myself in size, or which I apprehend by touch, were great or white or hot, it could not become different by mere contact with another unless it actually changed; nor again, if the comparing or apprehending subject were great or white or hot, could this, when unchanged from within, become changed by any approximation or affection of any other thing. The fact is that in our ordinary way of speaking we allow ourselves to be driven into most ridiculous and wonderful contradictions, as Protagoras and all who take his line of argument would remark.

THEAETETUS: How? And of what sort do you mean?

c *SOCRATES*: A little instance will sufficiently explain my meaning: Here are six dice, which are more by a half when compared with four, and fewer by a half than twelve—they are more and also fewer. How can you or anyone maintain the contrary?

THEAETETUS: Very true.

SOCRATES: Well, then, suppose that Protagoras or someone asks whether anything can become greater or more if not by increasing, how would you answer him, Theaetetus?

THEAETETUS: I should say "No," Socrates, if I were to speak my mind in
d reference to this last question, and if I were not afraid of contradicting my former answer.

SOCRATES: Capital! Excellent! Spoken like an oracle, my boy! And if you reply "Yes," there will be a case for Euripides; for our tongue will be unconvinced, but not our mind. (In allusion to the well-known line of Euripides, Hippol.: *e gloss omomoch e de thren anomotos.*)

Theaetetus: Very true.

Socrates: The thoroughbred Sophists, who know all that can be known
about the mind, and argue only out of the superfluity of their wits,
would have had a regular sparring-match over this, and would have e
knocked their arguments together finely. But you and I, who have no
professional aims, only desire to see what is the mutual relation of
these principles—whether they are consistent with each or not.

Theaetetus: Yes, that would be my desire.

Socrates: And mine too. But since this is our feeling, and there is plenty
of time, why should we not calmly and patiently review our own 155a
thoughts, and thoroughly examine and see what these appearances in
us really are? If I am not mistaken, they will be described by us as follows: first, that nothing can become greater or less, either in number
or magnitude, while remaining equal to itself—you would agree?

Theaetetus: Yes.

Socrates: Secondly, that without addition or subtraction there is no increase or diminution of anything, but only equality.

Theaetetus: Quite true.

Socrates: Thirdly, that what was not before cannot be afterwards, without b
becoming and having become.

Theaetetus: Yes, truly.

Socrates: These three axioms, if I am not mistaken, are fighting with one
another in our minds in the case of the dice, or, again, in such a case
as this—if I were to say that I, who am of a certain height and taller
than you, may within a year, without gaining or losing in height, be not
so tall—not that I should have lost, but that you would have increased.
In such a case, I am afterwards what I once was not, and yet I have not c
become; for I could not have become without becoming, neither
could I have become less without losing somewhat of my height; and
I could give you ten thousand examples of similar contradictions, if
we admit them at all. I believe that you follow me, Theaetetus; for I
suspect that you have thought of these questions before now.

Theaetetus: Yes, Socrates, and I am amazed when I think of them; by the Gods I am! And I want to know what on earth they mean; and there are times when my head quite swims with the contemplation of them.

Socrates: I see, my dear Theaetetus, that Theodorus had a true insight d
into your nature when he said that you were a philosopher, for wonder is the feeling of a philosopher, and philosophy begins in wonder.
He was not a bad genealogist who said that Iris (the messenger of

heaven) is the child of Thaumas (wonder). But do you begin to see what is the explanation of this perplexity on the hypothesis which we attribute to Protagoras?

THEAETETUS: Not as yet.

SOCRATES: Then you will be obliged to me if I help you to unearth the hid-
e den "truth" of a famous man or school.

THEAETETUS: To be sure, I shall be very much obliged.

SOCRATES: Take a look round, then, and see that none of the uninitiated are listening. Now by the uninitiated I mean the people who believe in nothing but what they can grasp in their hands, and who will not allow that action or generation or anything invisible can have real existence.

156a *THEAETETUS*: Yes, indeed, Socrates, they are very hard and impenetrable mortals.

SOCRATES: Yes, my boy, outer barbarians. Far more ingenious are the brethren whose mysteries I am about to reveal to you. Their first principle is, that all is motion, and upon this all the affections of which we were just now speaking are supposed to depend: there is
b nothing but motion, which has two forms, one active and the other passive, both in endless number; and out of the union and friction of them there is generated a progeny endless in number, having two forms, sense and the object of sense, which are ever breaking forth and coming to the birth at the same moment. The senses are variously named hearing, seeing, smelling; there is the sense of heat, cold, pleasure, pain, desire, fear, and many more which have names, as well as innumerable others which are without them; each has its
c kindred object—each variety of color has a corresponding variety of sight, and so with sound and hearing, and with the rest of the senses and the objects akin to them. Do you see, Theaetetus, the bearings of this tale on the preceding argument?

THEAETETUS: Indeed I do not.

SOCRATES: Then attend, and I will try to finish the story. The purport is that all these things are in motion, as I was saying, and that this motion is of two kinds, a slower and a quicker; and the slower elements have their motions in the same place and with reference to
d things near them, and so they beget; but what is begotten is swifter, for it is carried to and fro, and moves from place to place. Apply this to sense: When the eye and the appropriate object meet together and give birth to whiteness and the sensation connatural with it, which could not have been given by either of them going elsewhere, then,

while the sight is flowing from the eye, whiteness proceeds from the
object which combines in producing the color; and so the eye is ful- e
filled with sight, and really sees, and becomes, not sight, but a seeing
eye; and the object which combined to form the color is fulfilled with
whiteness, and becomes not whiteness but a white thing, whether
wood or stone or whatever the object may be which happens to be
colored white. And this is true of all sensible objects, hard, warm, and 157a
the like, which are similarly to be regarded, as I was saying before, not
as having any absolute existence, but as being all of them of whatever
kind generated by motion in their intercourse with one another; for
of the agent and patient, as existing in separation, no trustworthy
conception, as they say, can be formed, for the agent has no existence
until united with the patient, and the patient has no existence until
united with the agent; and that which by uniting with something
becomes an agent, by meeting with some other thing is converted into
a patient. And from all these considerations, as I said at first, there b
arises a general reflection, that there is no one self-existent thing, but
everything is becoming and in relation; and being must be altogether
abolished, although from habit and ignorance we are compelled even
in this discussion to retain the use of the term. But great philosophers
tell us that we are not to allow either the word "something," or
"belonging to something," or "to me," or "this," or "that," or any other
detaining name to be used, in the language of nature all things are
being created and destroyed, coming into being and passing into new
forms; nor can any name fix or detain them; he who attempts to fix
them is easily refuted. And this should be the way of speaking, not
only of particulars but of aggregates; such aggregates as are expressed
in the word "man," or "stone," or any name of an animal or of a class. c
O Theaetetus, are not these speculations sweet as honey? And do you
not like the taste of them in the mouth?

THEAETETUS: I do not know what to say, Socrates; for, indeed, I cannot make out whether you are giving your own opinion or only wanting to draw me out.

SOCRATES: You forget, my friend, that I neither know, nor profess to know,
anything of these matters; you are the person who is in labor, I am the
barren midwife; and this is why I soothe you, and offer you one good
thing after another, that you may taste them. And I hope that I may at d
last help to bring your own opinion into the light of day: when this has
been accomplished, then we will determine whether what you have

brought forth is only a wind-egg or a real and genuine birth. Therefore, keep up your spirits, and answer like a man what you think.

THEAETETUS: Ask me.

SOCRATES: Then once more: Is it your opinion that nothing is but what becomes? The good and the noble, as well as all the other things which we were just now mentioning?

THEAETETUS: When I hear you discoursing in this style, I think that there is a great deal in what you say, and I am very ready to assent.

e *SOCRATES*: Let us not leave the argument unfinished, then; for there still remains to be considered an objection which may be raised about dreams and diseases, in particular about madness, and the various illusions of hearing and sight, or of other senses. For you know that in all
158a these cases the esse-percipi theory appears to be unmistakably refuted, since in dreams and illusions we certainly have false perceptions; and far from saying that everything is which appears, we should rather say that nothing is which appears.

THEAETETUS: Very true, Socrates.

SOCRATES: But then, my boy, how can anyone contend that knowledge is perception, or that to every man what appears is?

THEAETETUS: I am afraid to say, Socrates, that I have nothing to answer, because you rebuked me just now for making this excuse; but I certainly cannot undertake to argue that madmen or dreamers think
b truly, when they imagine, some of them that they are gods, and others that they can fly, and are flying in their sleep.

SOCRATES: Do you see another question which can be raised about these phenomena, notably about dreaming and waking?

THEAETETUS: What question?

SOCRATES: A question which I think that you must often have heard persons ask: How can you determine whether at this moment we are sleeping,
c and all our thoughts are a dream; or whether we are awake, and talking to one another in the waking state?

THEAETETUS: Indeed, Socrates, I do not know how to prove the one any more than the other, for in both cases the facts precisely correspond; and there is no difficulty in supposing that during all this discussion we have been talking to one another in a dream; and when in a dream we seem to be narrating dreams, the resemblance of the two states is quite astonishing.

SOCRATES: You see, then, that a doubt about the reality of sense is easily raised, since there may even be a doubt whether we are awake or in

a dream. And as our time is equally divided between sleeping and d
waking, in either sphere of existence the soul contends that the thoughts which are present to our minds at the time are true; and during one half of our lives we affirm the truth of the one, and, during the other half, of the other; and are equally confident of both.

THEAETETUS: Most true.

SOCRATES: And may not the same be said of madness and other disorders? The difference is only that the times are not equal.

THEAETETUS: Certainly.

SOCRATES: And is truth or falsehood to be determined by duration of time?

THEAETETUS: That would be in many ways ridiculous. e

SOCRATES: But can you certainly determine by any other means which of these opinions is true?

THEAETETUS: I do not think that I can.

SOCRATES: Listen, then, to a statement of the other side of the argument, which is made by the champions of appearance. They would say, as I imagine—Can that which is wholly other than something, have the same quality as that from which it differs? And observe, Theaetetus, that the word "other" means not "partially," but "wholly other."

THEAETETUS: Certainly, putting the question as you do, that which is wholly 159a
other cannot either potentially or in any other way be the same.

SOCRATES: And must therefore be admitted to be unlike?

THEAETETUS: True.

SOCRATES: If, then, anything happens to become like or unlike itself or another, when it becomes like we call it the same—when unlike, other?

THEAETETUS: Certainly.

SOCRATES: Were we not saying that there are agents many and infinite, and patients many and infinite?

THEAETETUS: Yes.

SOCRATES: And also that different combinations will produce results which are not the same, but different?

THEAETETUS: Certainly. b

SOCRATES: Let us take you and me, or anything as an example: There is Socrates in health, and Socrates sick—Are they like or unlike?

THEAETETUS: You mean to compare Socrates in health as a whole, and Socrates in sickness as a whole?

SOCRATES: Exactly; that is my meaning.

THEAETETUS: I answer, they are unlike.

SOCRATES: And if unlike, they are other?

THEAETETUS: Certainly.

c *SOCRATES*: And would you not say the same of Socrates sleeping and waking, or in any of the states which we were mentioning?

THEAETETUS: I should.

SOCRATES: All agents have a different patient in Socrates, accordingly as he is well or ill.

THEAETETUS: Of course.

SOCRATES: And I who am the patient, and that which is the agent, will produce something different in each of the two cases?

THEAETETUS: Certainly.

SOCRATES: The wine which I drink when I am in health, appears sweet and pleasant to me?

THEAETETUS: True.

SOCRATES: For, as has been already acknowledged, the patient and agent
d meet together and produce sweetness and a perception of sweetness, which are in simultaneous motion, and the perception which comes from the patient makes the tongue percipient, and the quality of sweetness which arises out of and is moving about the wine, makes the wine both to be and to appear sweet to the healthy tongue.

THEAETETUS: Certainly; that has been already acknowledged.

SOCRATES: But when I am sick, the wine really acts upon another and a different person?

THEAETETUS: Yes.

e *SOCRATES*: The combination of the draught of wine, and the Socrates who is sick, produces quite another result; which is the sensation of bitterness in the tongue, and the motion and creation of bitterness in and about the wine, which becomes not bitterness but something bitter; as I myself become not perception but percipient?

THEAETETUS: True.

SOCRATES: There is no other object of which I shall ever have the same perception, for another object would give another perception, and would
160a make the percipient other and different; nor can that object which affects me, meeting another subject, produce the same, or become similar, for that too would produce another result from another subject, and become different.

THEAETETUS: True.

SOCRATES: Neither can I by myself, have this sensation, nor the object by itself, this quality.

THEAETETUS: Certainly not.

Socrates: When I perceive I must become percipient of something—there
can be no such thing as perceiving and perceiving nothing; the object, b
whether it become sweet, bitter, or of any other quality, must have
relation to a percipient; nothing can become sweet which is sweet to
no one.

Theaetetus: Certainly not.

Socrates: Then the inference is, that we (the agent and patient) are or
become in relation to one another; there is a law which binds us one
to the other, but not to any other existence, nor each of us to himself;
and therefore we can only be bound to one another; so that whether
a person says that a thing is or becomes, he must say that it is or
becomes to or of or in relation to something else; but he must not say c
or allow anyone else to say that anything is or becomes absolutely: such
is our conclusion.

Theaetetus: Very true, Socrates.

Socrates: Then, if that which acts upon me has relation to me and to no other, I and no other am the percipient of it?

Theaetetus: Of course.

Socrates: Then my perception is true to me, being inseparable from my own being; and, as Protagoras says, to myself I am judge of what is and what is not to me.

Theaetetus: I suppose so.

Socrates: How then, if I never err, and if my mind never trips in the concep- d
tion of being or becoming, can I fail of knowing that which I perceive?

Theaetetus: You cannot.

Socrates: Then you were quite right in affirming that knowledge is only
perception; and the meaning turns out to be the same, whether with
Homer and Heracleitus, and all that company, you say that all is
motion and flux, or with the great sage Protagoras, that man is the
measure of all things; or with Theaetetus, that, given these premises, e
perception is knowledge. Am I not right, Theaetetus, and is not this
your new-born child, of which I have delivered you? What say you?

Theaetetus: I cannot but agree, Socrates.

Socrates: Then this is the child, however he may turn out, which you and
I have with difficulty brought into the world. And now that he is born,
we must run round the hearth with him, and see whether he is worth
rearing, or is only a wind-egg and a sham. Is he to be reared in any 161a
case, and not exposed? Or will you bear to see him rejected, and not
get into a passion if I take away your firstborn?

THEODORUS: Theaetetus will not be angry, for he is very good-natured. But tell me, Socrates, in heaven's name, is this, after all, not the truth?

SOCRATES: You, Theodorus, are a lover of theories, and now you inno-
cently fancy that I am a bag full of them, and can easily pull one out
b which will overthrow its predecessor. But you do not see that in reality
none of these theories come from me; they all come from him who
talks with me. I only know just enough to extract them from the wisdom of another, and to receive them in a spirit of fairness. And now
I shall say nothing myself, but shall endeavor to elicit something from
our young friend.

THEODORUS: Do as you say, Socrates; you are quite right.

SOCRATES: Shall I tell you, Theodorus, what amazes me in your acquaintance Protagoras?

c *THEODORUS*: What is it?

SOCRATES: I am charmed with his doctrine, that what appears is to each
one, but I wonder that he did not begin his book on Truth with a
declaration that a pig or a dog-faced baboon, or some other yet
d stranger monster which has sensation, is the measure of all things;
then he might have shown a magnificent contempt for our opinion of
him by informing us at the outset that while we were reverencing him
like a God for his wisdom he was no better than a tadpole, not to
speak of his fellow-men—would not this have produced an overpow-
ering effect? For if truth is only sensation, and no man can discern
another's feelings better than he, or has any superior right to determine whether his opinion is true or false, but each, as we have several
times repeated, is to himself the sole judge, and everything that he
e judges is true and right, why, my friend, should Protagoras be preferred to the place of wisdom and instruction, and deserve to be well
paid, and we poor ignoramuses have to go to him, if each one is the
measure of his own wisdom? Must he not be talking "*ad captandum*" in
all this? I say nothing of the ridiculous predicament in which my own
midwifery and the whole art of dialectic is placed; for the attempt to
supervise or refute the notions or opinions of others would be a
tedious and enormous piece of folly, if to each man his own are right;
162a and this must be the case if Protagoras' Truth is the real truth, and
the philosopher is not merely amusing himself by giving oracles out
of the shrine of his book.

THEODORUS: He was a friend of mine, Socrates, as you were saying, and therefore I cannot have him refuted by my lips, nor can I oppose you when I agree with you; please, then, to take Theaetetus again; he seemed to answer very nicely.

SOCRATES: If you were to go into a Lacedaemonian palestra, Theodorus, b
would you have a right to look on at the naked wrestlers, some of them making a poor figure, if you did not strip and give them an opportunity of judging of your own person?

THEODORUS: Why not, Socrates, if they would allow me, as I think you will, in consideration of my age and stiffness; let some more supple youth try a fall with you, and do not drag me into the gymnasium.

SOCRATES: Your will is my will, Theodorus, as the proverbial philosophers say, and therefore I will return to the sage Theaetetus: Tell me, The- c
aetetus, in reference to what I was saying, are you not lost in wonder, like myself, when you find that all of a sudden you are raised to the level of the wisest of men, or indeed of the gods? For you would assume the measure of Protagoras to apply to the gods as well as men?

THEAETETUS: Certainly I should, and I confess to you that I am lost in wonder. At first hearing, I was quite satisfied with the doctrine, that whatever appears is to each one, but now the face of things has changed. d

SOCRATES: Why, my dear boy, you are young, and therefore your ear is quickly caught and your mind influenced by popular arguments. Protagoras, or someone speaking on his behalf, will doubtless say in reply—Good people, young and old, you meet and harangue, and e
bring in the gods, whose existence or nonexistence I banish from writing and speech, or you talk about the reason of man being degraded to the level of the brutes, which is a telling argument with the multitude, but not one word of proof or demonstration do you offer. All is probability with you, and yet surely you and Theodorus had better reflect whether you are disposed to admit of probability and figures of speech in matters of such importance. He or any other mathematician who argued from probabilities and likelihoods in geometry, would not 163a
be worth an ace.

THEAETETUS: But neither you nor we, Socrates, would be satisfied with such arguments.

SOCRATES: Then you and Theodorus mean to say that we must look at the matter in some other way?

THEAETETUS: Yes, in quite another way.

SOCRATES: And the way will be to ask whether perception is or is not the same as knowledge; for this was the real point of our argument, and with a view to this we raised (did we not?) those many strange questions.

THEAETETUS: Certainly.

b *SOCRATES*: Shall we say that we know everything which we see and hear? For example, shall we say that not having learned, we do not hear the language of foreigners when they speak to us? Or shall we say that we not only hear, but know what they are saying? Or again, if we see letters which we do not understand, shall we say that we do not see them? Or shall we aver that, seeing them, we must know them?

THEAETETUS: We shall say, Socrates, that we know what we actually see and hear of them—that is to say, we see and know the figure and color of
c the letters, and we hear and know the elevation or depression of the sound of them; but we do not perceive by sight and hearing, or know, that which grammarians and interpreters teach about them.

SOCRATES: Capital, Theaetetus; and about this there shall be no dispute, because I want you to grow; but there is another difficulty coming, which you will also have to repulse.

THEAETETUS: What is it?

d *SOCRATES*: Someone will say, Can a man who has ever known anything, and still has and preserves a memory of that which he knows, not know that which he remembers at the time when he remembers? I have, I fear, a tedious way of putting a simple question, which is only, whether a man who has learned, and remembers, can fail to know?

THEAETETUS: Impossible, Socrates; the supposition is monstrous.

SOCRATES: Am I talking nonsense, then? Think: is not seeing perceiving, and is not sight perception?

THEAETETUS: True.

e *SOCRATES*: And if our recent definition holds, every man knows that which he has seen?

THEAETETUS: Yes.

SOCRATES: And you would admit that there is such a thing as memory?

THEAETETUS: Yes.

SOCRATES: And is memory of something or of nothing?

THEAETETUS: Of something, surely.

SOCRATES: Of things learned and perceived, that is?

THEAETETUS: Certainly.

SOCRATES: Often a man remembers that which he has seen?

THEAETETUS: True.

SOCRATES: And if he closed his eyes, would he forget?

THEAETETUS: Who, Socrates, would dare to say so?

164a *SOCRATES*: But we must say so, if the previous argument is to be maintained.

Theaetetus: What do you mean? I am not quite sure that I understand you, though I have a strong suspicion that you are right.

Socrates: As thus: he who sees knows, as we say, that which he sees; for perception and sight and knowledge are admitted to be the same.

Theaetetus: Certainly.

Socrates: But he who saw, and has knowledge of that which he saw, remembers, when he closes his eyes, that which he no longer sees.

Theaetetus: True.

Socrates: And seeing is knowing, and therefore not-seeing is not-knowing? b

Theaetetus: Very true.

Socrates: Then the inference is, that a man may have attained the knowledge of something, which he may remember and yet not know, because he does not see; and this has been affirmed by us to be a monstrous supposition.

Theaetetus: Most true.

Socrates: Thus, then, the assertion that knowledge and perception are one, involves a manifest impossibility?

Theaetetus: Yes.

Socrates: Then they must be distinguished?

Theaetetus: I suppose that they must.

Socrates: Once more we shall have to begin, and ask "What is knowledge?" c
and yet, Theaetetus, what are we going to do?

Theaetetus: About what?

Socrates: Like a good-for-nothing cock, without having won the victory, we walk away from the argument and crow.

Theaetetus: How do you mean?

Socrates: After the manner of disputers (Lys.; Phaedo; Republic), we were
satisfied with mere verbal consistency, and were well pleased if in this
way we could gain an advantage. Although professing not to be mere
Eristics, but philosophers, I suspect that we have unconsciously fallen d
into the error of that ingenious class of persons.

Theaetetus: I do not as yet understand you.

Socrates: Then I will try to explain myself: just now we asked the question, whether a man who had learned and remembered could fail to know, and we showed that a person who had seen might remember when he had his eyes shut and could not see, and then he would at the same time remember and not know. But this was an impossibility. And so the Protagorean fable came to nought, and yours also, who maintained that knowledge is the same as perception.

e *THEAETETUS*: True.

SOCRATES: And yet, my friend, I rather suspect that the result would have been different if Protagoras, who was the father of the first of the two brats, had been alive; he would have had a great deal to say on their behalf. But he is dead, and we insult over his orphan child; and even the guardians whom he left, and of whom our friend Theodorus is one, are unwilling to give any help, and therefore I suppose that I must take up his cause myself, and see justice done?

165a *THEODORUS*: Not I, Socrates, but rather Callias, the son of Hipponicus, is guardian of his orphans. I was too soon diverted from the abstractions of dialectic to geometry. Nevertheless, I shall be grateful to you if you assist him.

SOCRATES: Very good, Theodorus; you shall see how I will come to the rescue. If a person does not attend to the meaning of terms as they are commonly used in argument, he may be involved even in greater paradoxes than these. Shall I explain this matter to you or to Theaetetus?

b *THEODORUS*: To both of us, and let the younger answer; he will incur less disgrace if he is discomfited.

SOCRATES: Then now let me ask the awful question, which is this: Can a man know and also not know that which he knows?

THEODORUS: How shall we answer, Theaetetus?

THEAETETUS: He cannot, I should say.

SOCRATES: He can, if you maintain that seeing is knowing. When you are imprisoned in a well, as the saying is, and the self-assured adversary closes one of your eyes with his hand, and asks whether you can see
c his cloak with the eye which he has closed, how will you answer the inevitable man?

THEAETETUS: I should answer, "Not with that eye but with the other."

SOCRATES: Then you see and do not see the same thing at the same time.

THEAETETUS: Yes, in a certain sense.

SOCRATES: None of that, he will reply; I do not ask or bid you answer in what sense you know, but only whether you know that which you do not know. You have been proved to see that which you do not see; and you have already admitted that seeing is knowing, and that not-seeing is not-knowing: I leave you to draw the inference.

d *THEAETETUS*: Yes; the inference is the contradictory of my assertion.

SOCRATES: Yes, my marvel, and there might have been yet worse things in store for you, if an opponent had gone on to ask whether you can have a sharp and also a dull knowledge, and whether you can know near,

but not at a distance, or know the same thing with more or less intensity, and so on without end. Such questions might have been put to you
by a light-armed mercenary, who argued for pay. He would have lain
in wait for you, and when you took up the position, that sense is knowledge, he would have made an assault upon hearing, smelling, and the e
other senses; he would have shown you no mercy; and while you were
lost in envy and admiration of his wisdom, he would have got you into
his net, out of which you would not have escaped until you had come
to an understanding about the sum to be paid for your release. Well,
you ask, and how will Protagoras reinforce his position? Shall I answer
for him?

Theaetetus: By all means.

Socrates: He will repeat all those things which we have been urging on his
behalf, and then he will close with us in disdain, and say: The worthy 166a
Socrates asked a little boy, whether the same man could remember
and not know the same thing, and the boy said No, because he was
frightened, and could not see what was coming, and then Socrates
made fun of poor me. The truth is, O slatternly Socrates, that when
you ask questions about any assertion of mine, and the person asked is
found tripping, if he has answered as I should have answered, then I b
am refuted, but if he answers something else, then he is refuted and
not I. For do you really suppose that anyone would admit the memory
which a man has of an impression which has passed away to be the
same with that which he experienced at the time? Assuredly not. Or
would he hesitate to acknowledge that the same man may know and
not know the same thing? Or, if he is afraid of making this admission,
would he ever grant that one who has become unlike is the same as
before he became unlike? Or would he admit that a man is one at all,
and not rather many and infinite as the changes which take place in
him? I speak by the card in order to avoid entanglements of words. c
But, O my good sir, he will say, come to the argument in a more generous spirit; and either show, if you can, that our sensations are not
relative and individual, or, if you admit them to be so, prove that this
does not involve the consequence that the appearance becomes, or,
if you will have the word, is, to the individual only. As to your talk
about pigs and baboons, you are yourself behaving like a pig, and you
teach your hearers to make sport of my writings in the same ignorant d
manner; but this is not to your credit. For I declare that the truth is as
I have written, and that each of us is a measure of existence and of

non-existence. Yet one man may be a thousand times better than
another in proportion as different things are and appear to him. And
I am far from saying that wisdom and the wise man have no existence;
but I say that the wise man is he who makes the evils which appear and
are to a man, into goods which are and appear to him. And I would
beg you not to press my words in the letter, but to take the meaning of
e them as I will explain them. Remember what has been already said—
that to the sick man his food appears to be and is bitter, and to the
man in health the opposite of bitter. Now I cannot conceive that one
167a of these men can be or ought to be made wiser than the other: nor can
you assert that the sick man because he has one impression is foolish,
and the healthy man because he has another is wise; but the one state
requires to be changed into the other, the worse into the better. As in
education, a change of state has to be effected, and the sophist accom-
plishes by words the change which the physician works by the aid of
drugs. Not that anyone ever made another think truly, who previously
thought falsely. For no one can think what is not, or, think anything
different from that which he feels; and this is always true. But as the
inferior habit of mind has thoughts of kindred nature, so I conceive
b that a good mind causes men to have good thoughts; and these
which the inexperienced call true, I maintain to be only better, and
not truer than others. And, O my dear Socrates, I do not call wise men
tadpoles: far from it; I say that they are the physicians of the human
c body, and the husbandmen of plants—for the husbandmen also take
away the evil and disordered sensations of plants, and infuse into
them good and healthy sensations—aye and true ones; and the wise
and good rhetoricians make the good instead of the evil to seem just
to states; for whatever appears to a state to be just and fair, so long as
it is regarded as such, is just and fair to it; but the teacher of wisdom
causes the good to take the place of the evil, both in appearance and in
d reality. And in like manner the Sophist who is able to train his pupils
in this spirit is a wise man, and deserves to be well paid by them. And
so one man is wiser than another; and no one thinks falsely, and you,
whether you will or not, must endure to be a measure. On these foun-
dations the argument stands firm, which you, Socrates, may, if you
please, overthrow by an opposite argument, or if you like you may put
questions to me—a method to which no intelligent person will object,
quite the reverse. But I must beg you to put fair questions: for there is
great inconsistency in saying that you have a zeal for virtue, and then

always behaving unfairly in argument. The unfairness of which I com- e
plain is that you do not distinguish between mere disputation and
dialectic: the disputer may trip up his opponent as often as he likes,
and make fun; but the dialectician will be in earnest, and only correct
his adversary when necessary, telling him the errors into which he 168a
has fallen through his own fault, or that of the company which he has
previously kept. If you do so, your adversary will lay the blame of his
own confusion and perplexity on himself, and not on you. He will follow and love you, and will hate himself, and escape from himself into
philosophy, in order that he may become different from what he was.
But the other mode of arguing, which is practiced by the many, will
have just the opposite effect upon him; and as he grows older, instead
of turning philosopher, he will come to hate philosophy. I would rec- b
ommend you, therefore, as I said before, not to encourage yourself in
this polemical and controversial temper, but to find out, in a friendly
and congenial spirit, what we really mean when we say that all things
are in motion, and that to every individual and state what appears, is.
In this manner you will consider whether knowledge and sensation are
the same or different, but you will not argue, as you were just now
doing, from the customary use of names and words, which the vulgar c
pervert in all sorts of ways, causing infinite perplexity to one another.
Such, Theodorus, is the very slight help which I am able to offer to
your old friend; had he been living, he would have helped himself in
a far more gloriose style.

THEODORUS: You are jesting, Socrates; indeed, your defense of him has been most valorous.

SOCRATES: Thank you, friend; and I hope that you observed Protagoras bid-
ding us be serious, as the text, "Man is the measure of all things," was
a solemn one; and he reproached us with making a boy the medium d
of discourse, and said that the boy's timidity was made to tell against
his argument; he also declared that we made a joke of him.

THEODORUS: How could I fail to observe all that, Socrates?

SOCRATES: Well, and shall we do as he says?

THEODORUS: By all means.

SOCRATES: But if his wishes are to be regarded, you and I must take up the
argument, and in all seriousness, and ask and answer one another, for
you see that the rest of us are nothing but boys. In no other way can e
we escape the imputation, that in our fresh analysis of his thesis we are
making fun with boys.

THEODORUS: Well, but is not Theaetetus better able to follow a philosophical enquiry than a great many men who have long beards?

SOCRATES: Yes, Theodorus, but not better than you; and therefore please
not to imagine that I am to defend by every means in my power your
169a departed friend; and that you are to defend nothing and nobody. At
any rate, my good man, do not sheer off until we know whether you are
a true measure of diagrams, or whether all men are equally measures
and sufficient for themselves in astronomy and geometry, and the other
branches of knowledge in which you are supposed to excel them.

THEODORUS: He who is sitting by you, Socrates, will not easily avoid being
drawn into an argument; and when I said just now that you would
excuse me, and not, like the Lacedaemonians, compel me to strip and
b fight, I was talking nonsense—I should rather compare you to Scir-
rhon, who threw travelers from the rocks; for the Lacedaemonian rule
is "strip or depart," but you seem to go about your work more after the
fashion of Antaeus: you will not allow anyone who approaches you to
depart until you have stripped him, and he has been compelled to try
a fall with you in argument.

SOCRATES: There, Theodorus, you have hit off precisely the nature of my
complaint; but I am even more pugnacious than the giants of old, for
I have met with no end of heroes; many a Heracles, many a Theseus,
mighty in words, has broken my head; nevertheless I am always at this
c rough exercise, which inspires me like a passion. Please, then, to try a
fall with me, whereby you will do yourself good as well as me.

THEODORUS: I consent; lead me whither you will, for I know that you are like destiny; no man can escape from any argument which you may weave for him. But I am not disposed to go further than you suggest.

SOCRATES: Once will be enough; and now take particular care that we do not
d again unwittingly expose ourselves to the reproach of talking childishly.

THEODORUS: I will do my best to avoid that error.

SOCRATES: In the first place, let us return to our old objection, and see whether we were right in blaming and taking offense at Protagoras on the ground that he assumed all to be equal and sufficient in wisdom; although he admitted that there was a better and worse, and that in respect of this, some who as he said were the wise excelled others.

THEODORUS: Very true.

SOCRATES: Had Protagoras been living and answered for himself, instead of
e our answering for him, there would have been no need of our review-
ing or reinforcing the argument. But as he is not here, and someone

may accuse us of speaking without authority on his behalf, had we not better come to a clearer agreement about his meaning, for a great deal may be at stake?

THEODORUS: True.

SOCRATES: Then let us obtain, not through any third person, but from his
own statement and in the fewest words possible, the basis of agreement. 170a

THEODORUS: In what way?

SOCRATES: In this way: His words are, "What seems to a man, is to him."

THEODORUS: Yes, so he says.

SOCRATES: And are not we, Protagoras, uttering the opinion of man, or rather of all mankind, when we say that everyone thinks himself wiser than other men in some things, and their inferior in others? In the hour of danger, when they are in perils of war, or of the sea, or of sickness, do they not look up to their commanders as if they were gods,
and expect salvation from them, only because they excel them in b
knowledge? Is not the world full of men in their several employments, who are looking for teachers and rulers of themselves and of the animals? And there are plenty who think that they are able to teach and able to rule. Now, in all this is implied that ignorance and wisdom exist among them, at least in their own opinion.

THEODORUS: Certainly.

SOCRATES: And wisdom is assumed by them to be true thought, and ignorance to be false opinion.

THEODORUS: Exactly. c

SOCRATES: How then, Protagoras, would you have us treat the argument? Shall we say that the opinions of men are always true, or sometimes true and sometimes false? In either case, the result is the same, and their opinions are not always true, but sometimes true and sometimes false. For tell me, Theodorus, do you suppose that you yourself, or any other follower of Protagoras, would contend that no one deems another ignorant or mistaken in his opinion?

THEODORUS: The thing is incredible, Socrates.

SOCRATES: And yet that absurdity is necessarily involved in the thesis which d
declares man to be the measure of all things.

THEODORUS: How so?

SOCRATES: Why, suppose that you determine in your own mind something to be true, and declare your opinion to me; let us assume, as he argues, that this is true to you. Now, if so, you must either say that the rest of us are not the judges of this opinion or judgment of yours, or that we judge you always to have a true opinion? But are there not thousands upon thousands who, whenever you form a judgment, take up arms against you and are of an opposite judgment and opinion, deeming that you judge falsely?

e *THEODORUS*: Yes, indeed, Socrates, thousands and tens of thousands, as Homer says, who give me a world of trouble.

SOCRATES: Well, but are we to assert that what you think is true to you and false to the ten thousand others?

THEODORUS: No other inference seems to be possible.

SOCRATES: And how about Protagoras himself? If neither he nor the multitude thought, as indeed they do not think, that man is the measure of all things, must it not follow that the truth of which Protagoras wrote
171a would be true to no one? But if you suppose that he himself thought this, and that the multitude does not agree with him, you must begin by allowing that in whatever proportion the many are more than one, in that proportion his truth is more untrue than true.

THEODORUS: That would follow if the truth is supposed to vary with individual opinion.

SOCRATES: And the best of the joke is, that he acknowledges the truth of their opinion who believe his own opinion to be false; for he admits that the opinions of all men are true.

THEODORUS: Certainly.

b *SOCRATES*: And does he not allow that his own opinion is false, if he admits that the opinion of those who think him false is true?

THEODORUS: Of course.

SOCRATES: Whereas the other side do not admit that they speak falsely?

THEODORUS: They do not.

SOCRATES: And he, as may be inferred from his writings, agrees that this opinion is also true.

THEODORUS: Clearly.

SOCRATES: Then all mankind, beginning with Protagoras, will contend, or rather, I should say that he will allow, when he concedes that his adver-
c sary has a true opinion—Protagoras, I say, will himself allow that neither a dog nor any ordinary man is the measure of anything which he has not learned—am I not right?

THEODORUS: Yes.

SOCRATES: And the truth of Protagoras being doubted by all, will be true neither to himself to anyone else?

THEODORUS: I think, Socrates, that we are running my old friend too hard.

Socrates: But I do not know that we are going beyond the truth. Doubtless,
as he is older, he may be expected to be wiser than we are. And if he d
could only just get his head out of the world below, he would have
overthrown both of us again and again, me for talking nonsense and
you for assenting to me, and have been off and underground in a trice.
But as he is not within call, we must make the best use of our own
faculties, such as they are, and speak out what appears to us to be true.
And one thing which no one will deny is, that there are great differences in the understandings of men.

Theodorus: In that opinion I quite agree.

Socrates: And is there not most likely to be firm ground in the distinction
which we were indicating on behalf of Protagoras, viz. that most things, e
and all immediate sensations, such as hot, dry, sweet, are only such as
they appear; if however difference of opinion is to be allowed at all,
surely we must allow it in respect of health or disease? For every
woman, child, or living creature has not such a knowledge of what
conduces to health as to enable them to cure themselves.

Theodorus: I quite agree.

Socrates: Or again, in politics, while affirming that just and unjust, honor- 172a
able and disgraceful, holy and unholy, are in reality to each state such
as the state thinks and makes lawful, and that in determining these
matters no individual or state is wiser than another, still the followers
of Protagoras will not deny that in determining what is or is not expe- b
dient for the community one state is wiser and one counsellor better
than another—they will scarcely venture to maintain, that what a city
enacts in the belief that it is expedient will always be really expedient.
But in the other case, I mean when they speak of justice and injustice,
piety and impiety, they are confident that in nature these have no
existence or essence of their own—the truth is that which is agreed on
at the time of the agreement, and as long as the agreement lasts; and
this is the philosophy of many who do not altogether go along with
Protagoras. Here arises a new question, Theodorus, which threatens to c
be more serious than the last.

Theodorus: Well, Socrates, we have plenty of leisure.

Socrates: That is true, and your remark recalls to my mind an observation which I have often made, that those who have passed their days in the pursuit of philosophy are ridiculously at fault when they have to appear and speak in court. How natural is this!

Theodorus: What do you mean?

Socrates: I mean to say, that those who have been trained in philosophy
and liberal pursuits are as unlike those who from their youth upwards
d have been knocking about in the courts and such places, as a freeman
is in breeding unlike a slave.

Theodorus: In what is the difference seen?

Socrates: In the leisure spoken of by you, which a freeman can always command: he has his talk out in peace, and, like ourselves, he wanders at
will from one subject to another, and from a second to a third—if the
fancy takes him, he begins again, as we are doing now, caring not
whether his words are many or few; his only aim is to attain the truth.
But the lawyer is always in a hurry; there is the water of the clepsydra
driving him on, and not allowing him to expatiate at will: and there is
e his adversary standing over him, enforcing his rights; the indictment,
which in their phraseology is termed the affidavit, is recited at the
time: and from this he must not deviate. He is a servant, and is continually disputing about a fellow-servant before his master, who is
seated, and has the cause in his hands; the trial is never about some
indifferent matter, but always concerns himself; and often the race is
for his life. The consequence has been, that he has become keen and
shrewd; he has learned how to flatter his master in word and indulge
him in deed; but his soul is small and unrighteous. His condition,
which has been that of a slave from his youth upwards, has deprived
him of growth and uprightness and independence; dangers and fears,
173a which were too much for his truth and honesty, came upon him in
early years, when the tenderness of youth was unequal to them, and he
has been driven into crooked ways; from the first he has practiced
b deception and retaliation, and has become stunted and warped. And
so he has passed out of youth into manhood, having no soundness in
him; and is now, as he thinks, a master in wisdom. Such is the lawyer,
Theodorus. Will you have the companion picture of the philosopher,
who is of our brotherhood; or shall we return to the argument? Do not
let us abuse the freedom of digression which we claim.

Theodorus: Nay, Socrates, not until we have finished what we are about;
c for you truly said that we belong to a brotherhood which is free, and
are not the servants of the argument; but the argument is our servant,
and must wait our leisure. Who is our judge? Or where is the spectator
having any right to censure or control us, as he might the poets?

Socrates: Then, as this is your wish, I will describe the leaders; for there is
no use in talking about the inferior sort. In the first place, the lords of

philosophy have never, from their youth upwards, known their way
to the Agora, or the dicastery, or the council, or any other political d
assembly; they neither see nor hear the laws or decrees, as they are
called, of the state written or recited; the eagerness of political societ-
ies in the attainment of offices—clubs, and banquets, and revels, and
singing-maidens—do not enter even into their dreams. Whether any
event has turned out well or ill in the city, what disgrace may have
descended to anyone from his ancestors, male or female, are matters
of which the philosopher no more knows than he can tell, as they say,
how many pints are contained in the ocean. Neither is he conscious of e
his ignorance. For he does not hold aloof in order that he may gain a
reputation; but the truth is, that the outer form of him only is in the
city: his mind, disdaining the littlenesses and nothingnesses of human
things, is "flying all abroad" as Pindar says, measuring earth and
heaven and the things which are under and on the earth and above
the heaven, interrogating the whole nature of each and all in their
entirety, but not condescending to anything which is within reach. 174a

THEODORUS: What do you mean, Socrates?

SOCRATES: I will illustrate my meaning, Theodorus, by the jest which the
clever witty Thracian handmaid is said to have made about Thales,
when he fell into a well as he was looking up at the stars. She said, that
he was so eager to know what was going on in heaven, that he could not
see what was before his feet. This is a jest which is equally applicable to
all philosophers. For the philosopher is wholly unacquainted with his b
next-door neighbor; he is ignorant, not only of what he is doing, but he
hardly knows whether he is a man or an animal; he is searching into the
essence of man, and busy in enquiring what belongs to such a nature
to do or suffer different from any other; I think that you understand
me, Theodorus?

THEODORUS: I do, and what you say is true.

SOCRATES: And thus, my friend, on every occasion, private as well as public,
as I said at first, when he appears in a law-court, or in any place in c
which he has to speak of things which are at his feet and before his
eyes, he is the jest, not only of Thracian handmaids but of the general
herd, tumbling into wells and every sort of disaster through his inex-
perience. His awkwardness is fearful, and gives the impression of
imbecility. When he is reviled, he has nothing personal to say in
answer to the civilities of his adversaries, for he knows no scandals of
anyone, and they do not interest him; and therefore he is laughed at

for his sheepishness; and when others are being praised and glorified,
d in the simplicity of his heart he cannot help going into fits of laugh-
ter, so that he seems to be a downright idiot. When he hears a tyrant
or king eulogized, he fancies that he is listening to the praises of some
keeper of cattle—a swineherd, or shepherd, or perhaps a cowherd,
who is congratulated on the quantity of milk which he squeezes from
them; and he remarks that the creature whom they tend, and out of
whom they squeeze the wealth, is of a less tractable and more insidi-
ous nature. Then, again, he observes that the great man is of necessity
as ill-mannered and uneducated as any shepherd—for he has no lei-
e sure, and he is surrounded by a wall, which is his mountain-pen.
Hearing of enormous landed proprietors of ten thousand acres and
more, our philosopher deems this to be a trifle, because he has been
accustomed to think of the whole earth; and when they sing the praises
of family, and say that someone is a gentleman because he can show
seven generations of wealthy ancestors, he thinks that their senti-
ments only betray a dull and narrow vision in those who utter them,
175a and who are not educated enough to look at the whole, nor to consider
that every man has had thousands and ten thousands of progeni-
tors, and among them have been rich and poor, kings and slaves,
Hellenes and barbarians, innumerable. And when people pride themselves on having a pedigree of twenty-five ancestors, which goes back
to Heracles, the son of Amphitryon, he cannot understand their pov-
b erty of ideas. Why are they unable to calculate that Amphitryon had a
twenty-fifth ancestor, who might have been anybody, and was such as
fortune made him, and he had a fiftieth, and so on? He amuses himself with the notion that they cannot count, and thinks that a little
arithmetic would have got rid of their senseless vanity. Now, in all
these cases our philosopher is derided by the vulgar, partly because
he is thought to despise them, and also because he is ignorant of what
is before him, and always at a loss.

THEODORUS: That is very true, Socrates.

SOCRATES: But, O my friend, when he draws the other into upper air, and
gets him out of his pleas and rejoinders into the contemplation of
c justice and injustice in their own nature and in their difference from
one another and from all other things; or from the commonplaces
about the happiness of a king or of a rich man to the consideration of
government, and of human happiness and misery in general—what
they are, and how a man is to attain the one and avoid the other—

when that narrow, keen, little legal mind is called to account about all d
this, he gives the philosopher his revenge; for dizzied by the height at
which he is hanging, whence he looks down into space, which is a
strange experience to him, he being dismayed, and lost, and stammer-
ing broken words, is laughed at, not by Thracian handmaidens or any
other uneducated persons, for they have no eye for the situation, but
by every man who has not been brought up a slave. Such are the two e
characters, Theodorus: the one of the freeman, who has been trained
in liberty and leisure, whom you call the philosopher—him we cannot
blame because he appears simple and of no account when he has to
perform some menial task, such as packing up bedclothes, or flavoring
a sauce or fawning speech; the other character is that of the man who
is able to do all this kind of service smartly and neatly, but knows not
how to wear his cloak like a gentleman; still less with the music of discourse can he hymn the true life aright which is lived by immortals or 176a
men blessed of heaven.

THEODORUS: If you could only persuade everybody, Socrates, as you do me, of the truth of your words, there would be more peace and fewer evils among men.

SOCRATES: Evils, Theodorus, can never pass away; for there must always
remain something which is antagonistic to good. Having no place
among the gods in heaven, of necessity they hover around the mortal b
nature, and this earthly sphere. Wherefore we ought to fly away from
earth to heaven as quickly as we can; and to fly away is to become like
God, as far as this is possible; and to become like him, is to become c
holy, just, and wise. But, O my friend, you cannot easily convince mankind that they should pursue virtue or avoid vice, not merely in order
that a man may seem to be good, which is the reason given by the
world, and in my judgment is only a repetition of an old wives' fable.
Whereas, the truth is that God is never in any way unrighteous—he is
perfect righteousness; and he of us who is the most righteous is most
like him. Herein is seen the true cleverness of a man, and also his
nothingness and want of manhood. For to know this is true wisdom
and virtue, and ignorance of this is manifest folly and vice. All other
kinds of wisdom or cleverness, which seem only, such as the wisdom of
politicians, or the wisdom of the arts, are coarse and vulgar. The
unrighteous man, or the sayer and doer of unholy things, had far better not be encouraged in the illusion that his roguery is clever; for men d
glory in their shame—they fancy that they hear others saying of them,

"These are not mere good-for-nothing persons, mere burdens of the
earth, but such as men should be who mean to dwell safely in a state."
Let us tell them that they are all the more truly what they do not think
they are because they do not know it; for they do not know the penalty
of injustice, which above all things they ought to know—not stripes
e and death, as they suppose, which evildoers often escape, but a penalty
which cannot be escaped.

THEODORUS: What is that?

SOCRATES: There are two patterns eternally set before them; the one blessed
and divine, the other godless and wretched: but they do not see them,
or perceive that in their utter folly and infatuation they are growing
177a like the one and unlike the other, by reason of their evil deeds; and
the penalty is, that they lead a life answering to the pattern which
they are growing like. And if we tell them, that unless they depart
from their cunning, the place of innocence will not receive them
after death; and that here on earth, they will live ever in the likeness
of their own evil selves, and with evil friends—when they hear this
they in their superior cunning will seem to be listening to the talk
of idiots.

THEODORUS: Very true, Socrates.

b *SOCRATES*: Too true, my friend, as I well know; there is, however, one pecu-
liarity in their case: when they begin to reason in private about their
dislike of philosophy, if they have the courage to hear the argument
out, and do not run away, they grow at last strangely discontented with
themselves; their rhetoric fades away, and they become helpless as
children. These however are digressions from which we must now
c desist, or they will overflow, and drown the original argument; to
which, if you please, we will now return.

THEODORUS: For my part, Socrates, I would rather have the digressions, for at my age I find them easier to follow; but if you wish, let us go back to the argument.

SOCRATES: Had we not reached the point at which the partisans of the perpetual flux, who say that things are as they seem to each one, were
confidently maintaining that the ordinances which the state com-
d manded and thought just, were just to the state which imposed them,
while they were in force; this was especially asserted of justice; but
as to the good, no one had any longer the hardihood to contend of
any ordinances which the state thought and enacted to be good that
these, while they were in force, were really good; he who said so would

be playing with the name "good," and would not touch the real question—it would be a mockery, would it not?

THEODORUS: Certainly it would.

SOCRATES: He ought not to speak of the name, but of the thing which is e
contemplated under the name.

THEODORUS: Right.

SOCRATES: Whatever be the term used, the good or expedient is the aim of legislation, and as far as she has an opinion, the state imposes all laws with a view to the greatest expediency; can legislation have any other aim?

THEODORUS: Certainly not. 178a

SOCRATES: But is the aim attained always? Do not mistakes often happen?

THEODORUS: Yes, I think that there are mistakes.

SOCRATES: The possibility of error will be more distinctly recognized, if we put the question in reference to the whole class under which the good or expedient falls. That whole class has to do with the future, and laws are passed under the idea that they will be useful in after-time; which, in other words, is the future.

THEODORUS: Very true. b

SOCRATES: Suppose now, that we ask Protagoras, or one of his disciples, a question: O, Protagoras, we will say to him, Man is, as you declare, the measure of all things—white, heavy, light: of all such things he is the judge; for he has the criterion of them in himself, and when he thinks that things are such as he experiences them to be, he thinks what is and is true to himself. Is it not so?

THEODORUS: Yes.

SOCRATES: And do you extend your doctrine, Protagoras (as we shall further say), to the future as well as to the present; and has he the c
criterion not only of what in his opinion is but of what will be, and do things always happen to him as he expected? For example, take the case of heat: When an ordinary man thinks that he is going to have a fever, and that this kind of heat is coming on, and another person, who is a physician, thinks the contrary, whose opinion is likely to prove right? Or are they both right? He will have a heat and fever in his own judgment, and not have a fever in the physician's judgment?

THEODORUS: How ludicrous!

SOCRATES: And the vinegrower, if I am not mistaken, is a better judge of the
sweetness or dryness of the vintage which is not yet gathered than d
the harp-player?

Theodorus: Certainly.

Socrates: And in musical composition the musician will know better than the training master what the training master himself will hereafter think harmonious or the reverse?

Theodorus: Of course.

Socrates: And the cook will be a better judge than the guest, who is not a
e cook, of the pleasure to be derived from the dinner which is in prepara-
tion; for of present or past pleasure we are not as yet arguing; but can
we say that everyone will be to himself the best judge of the pleasure
which will seem to be and will be to him in the future? Nay, would not
you, Protagoras, better guess which arguments in a court would convince any one of us than the ordinary man?

Theodorus: Certainly, Socrates, he used to profess in the strongest manner that he was the superior of all men in this respect.

179a *Socrates*: To be sure, friend: who would have paid a large sum for the
privilege of talking to him, if he had really persuaded his visitors that
neither a prophet nor any other man was better able to judge what will
be and seem to be in the future than everyone could for himself?

Theodorus: Who indeed?

Socrates: And legislation and expediency are all concerned with the future; and everyone will admit that states, in passing laws, must often fail of their highest interests?

Theodorus: Quite true.

Socrates: Then we may fairly argue against your master, that he must
b admit one man to be wiser than another, and that the wiser is a measure: but I, who know nothing, am not at all obliged to accept the
honor which the advocate of Protagoras was just now forcing upon me,
whether I would or not, of being a measure of anything.

Theodorus: That is the best refutation of him, Socrates; although he is also caught when he ascribes truth to the opinions of others, who give the lie direct to his own opinion.

c *Socrates*: There are many ways, Theodorus, in which the doctrine that
every opinion of every man is true may be refuted; but there is more
difficulty in proving that states of feeling, which are present to a man,
and out of which arise sensations and opinions in accordance with
them, are also untrue. And very likely I have been talking nonsense
about them; for they may be unassailable, and those who say that there
is clear evidence of them, and that they are matters of knowledge,
may probably be right; in which case our friend Theaetetus was not so

far from the mark when he identified perception and knowledge. And d
therefore let us draw nearer, as the advocate of Protagoras desires;
and give the truth of the universal flux a ring: is the theory sound or
not? At any rate, no small war is raging about it, and there are combination not a few.

THEODORUS: No small, war, indeed, for in Ionia the sect makes rapid strides;
the disciples of Heracleitus are most energetic upholders of the doctrine.

SOCRATES: Then we are the more bound, my dear Theodorus, to examine
the question from the foundation as it is set forth by themselves. e

THEODORUS: Certainly we are. About these speculations of Heracleitus, which,
as you say, are as old as Homer, or even older still, the Ephesians themselves, who profess to know them, are downright mad, and you cannot
talk with them on the subject. For, in accordance with their textbooks,
they are always in motion; but as for dwelling upon an argument or a
question, and quietly asking and answering in turn, they can no more
do so than they can fly; or rather, the determination of these fellows not
to have a particle of rest in them is more than the utmost powers of
negation can express. If you ask any of them a question, he will pro- 180a
duce, as from a quiver, sayings brief and dark, and shoot them at you;
and if you inquire the reason of what he has said, you will be hit by
some other newfangled word, and will make no way with any of them,
nor they with one another; their great care is, not to allow of any settled
principle either in their arguments or in their minds, conceiving, as I b
imagine, that any such principle would be stationary; for they are at war
with the stationary, and do what they can to drive it out everywhere.

SOCRATES: I suppose, Theodorus, that you have only seen them when they
were fighting, and have never stayed with them in time of peace, for
they are no friends of yours; and their peace doctrines are only communicated by them at leisure, as I imagine, to those disciples of theirs
whom they want to make like themselves.

THEODORUS: Disciples! My good sir, they have none; men of their sort are
not one another's disciples, but they grow up at their own sweet will, c
and get their inspiration anywhere, each of them saying of his neighbor that he knows nothing. From these men, then, as I was going to
remark, you will never get a reason, whether with their will or without
their will; we must take the question out of their hands, and make the
analysis ourselves, as if we were doing geometrical problem.

SOCRATES: Quite right too; but as touching the aforesaid problem, have we
not heard from the ancients, who concealed their wisdom from the d

many in poetical figures, that Oceanus and Tethys, the origin of all things, are streams, and that nothing is at rest? And now the moderns, in their superior wisdom, have declared the same openly, that the cobbler too may hear and learn of them, and no longer foolishly imagine that some things are at rest and others in motion—having learned that all is motion, he will duly honor his teachers. I had almost forgotten
e the opposite doctrine, Theodorus,

Alone Being remains unmoved, which is the name for the all.

This is the language of Parmenides, Melissus, and their followers, who stoutly maintain that all being is one and self-contained, and has no place in which to move. What shall we do, friend, with all these people; for, advancing step by step, we have imperceptibly got between the combatants, and, unless we can protect our retreat, we shall pay the penalty of our rashness—like the players in the palaestra who are
181a caught upon the line, and are dragged different ways by the two parties. Therefore I think that we had better begin by considering those whom we first accosted, "the river-gods," and, if we find any truth in them, we will help them to pull us over, and try to get away from he others. But if the partisans of "the whole" appear to speak more truly, we will fly off from the party which would move the immovable, to them.
b And if I find that neither of them have anything reasonable to say, we shall be in a ridiculous position, having so great a conceit of our own poor opinion and rejecting that of ancient and famous men. O Theodorus, do you think that there is any use in proceeding when the danger is so great?

THEODORUS: Nay, Socrates, not to examine thoroughly what the two parties have to say would be quite intolerable.

SOCRATES: Then examine we must, since you, who were so reluctant to
c begin, are so eager to proceed. The nature of motion appears to be the question with which we begin. What do they mean when they say that all things are in motion? Is there only one kind of motion, or, as I rather incline to think, two? I should like to have your opinion upon this point in addition to my own, that I may err, if I must err, in your company; tell me, then, when a thing changes from one place to another, or goes round in the same place, is not that what is called motion?

Theodorus: Yes.

Socrates: Here then we have one kind of motion. But when a thing,
remaining on the same spot, grows old, or becomes black from being d
white, or hard from being soft, or undergoes any other change, may
not this be properly called motion of another kind?

Theodorus: I think so.

Socrates: Say rather that it must be so. Of motion then there are these two kinds, "change," and "motion in place."

Theodorus: You are right.

Socrates: And now, having made this distinction, let us address ourselves
to those who say that all is motion, and ask them whether all things e
according to them have the two kinds of motion, and are changed as
well as move in place, or is one thing moved in both ways, and another
in one only?

Theodorus: Indeed, I do not know what to answer; but I think they would say that all things are moved in both ways.

Socrates: Yes, comrade; for, if not, they would have to say that the same things are in motion and at rest, and there would be no more truth in saying that all things are in motion, than that all things are at rest.

Theodorus: To be sure.

Socrates: And if they are to be in motion, and nothing is to be devoid of 182a
motion, all things must always have every sort of motion?

Theodorus: Most true.

Socrates: Consider a further point: did we not understand them to
explain the generation of heat, whiteness, or anything else, in some
such manner as the following: were they not saying that each of them
is moving between the agent and the patient, together with a perception, and that the patient ceases to be a perceiving power and becomes
a percipient, and the agent a quale instead of a quality? I suspect that
quality may appear a strange and uncouth term to you, and that you
do not understand the abstract expression. Then I will take concrete b
instances: I mean to say that the producing power or agent becomes
neither heat nor whiteness but hot and white, and the like of other
things. For I must repeat what I said before, that neither the agent nor
patient have any absolute existence, but when they come together and
generate sensations and their objects, the one becomes a thing of a
certain quality, and the other a percipient. You remember?

Theodorus: Of course.

c *SOCRATES*: We may leave the details of their theory unexamined, but we must not forget to ask them the only question with which we are concerned: Are all things in motion and flux?

THEODORUS: Yes, they will reply.

SOCRATES: And they are moved in both those ways which we distinguished, that is to say, they move in place and are also changed?

THEODORUS: Of course, if the motion is to be perfect.

SOCRATES: If they only moved in place and were not changed, we should be able to say what is the nature of the things which are in motion and flux?

THEODORUS: Exactly.

d *SOCRATES*: But now, since not even white continues to flow white, and whiteness itself is a flux or change which is passing into another color, and is never to be caught standing still, can the name of any color be rightly used at all?

THEODORUS: How is that possible, Socrates, either in the case of this or of any other quality—if while we are using the word the object is escaping in the flux?

SOCRATES: And what would you say of perceptions, such as sight and hearing, or any other kind of perception? Is there any stopping in the act
e of seeing and hearing?

THEODORUS: Certainly not, if all things are in motion.

SOCRATES: Then we must not speak of seeing any more than of not-seeing, nor of any other perception more than of any non-perception, if all things partake of every kind of motion?

THEODORUS: Certainly not.

SOCRATES: Yet perception is knowledge: so at least Theaetetus and I were saying.

THEODORUS: Very true.

SOCRATES: Then when we were asked what is knowledge, we no more answered what is knowledge than what is not knowledge?

183a *THEODORUS*: I suppose not.

SOCRATES: Here, then, is a fine result: we corrected our first answer in our eagerness to prove that nothing is at rest. But if nothing is at rest, every answer upon whatever subject is equally right: you may say that a thing is or is not thus; or, if you prefer, "becomes" thus; and if we say "becomes," we shall not then hamper them with words expressive of rest.

THEODORUS: Quite true.

SOCRATES: Yes, Theodorus, except in saying "thus" and "not thus." But you
b ought not to use the word "thus," for there is no motion in "thus" or

in "not thus." The maintainers of the doctrine have as yet no words in which to express themselves, and must get a new language. I know of no word that will suit them, except perhaps "no how," which is perfectly indefinite.

THEODORUS: Yes, that is a manner of speaking in which they will be quite at home.

SOCRATES: And so, Theodorus, we have got rid of your friend without
assenting to his doctrine, that every man is the measure of all things— c
a wise man only is a measure; neither can we allow that knowledge is perception, certainly not on the hypothesis of a perpetual flux, unless perchance our friend Theaetetus is able to convince us that it is.

THEODORUS: Very good, Socrates; and now that the argument about the doctrine of Protagoras has been completed, I am absolved from answering; for this was the agreement.

THEAETETUS: Not, Theodorus, until you and Socrates have discussed the doctrine of those who say that all things are at rest, as you were proposing. d

THEODORUS: You, Theaetetus, who are a young rogue, must not instigate your elders to a breach of faith, but should prepare to answer Socrates in the remainder of the argument.

THEAETETUS: Yes, if he wishes; but I would rather have heard about the doctrine of rest.

THEODORUS: Invite Socrates to an argument—invite horsemen to the open plain; do but ask him, and he will answer.

SOCRATES: Nevertheless, Theodorus, I am afraid that I shall not be able to
comply with the request of Theaetetus. e

THEODORUS: Not comply! For what reason?

SOCRATES: My reason is that I have a kind of reverence; not so much for Melissus and the others, who say that "All is one and at rest," as for the great leader himself, Parmenides, venerable and awful, as in Homeric language he may be called; him I should be ashamed to approach in a spirit unworthy of him. I met him when he was an old man, and I was a mere youth, and he appeared to me to have a glorious depth of mind. And I am afraid that we may not understand his 184a
words, and may be still further from understanding his meaning; above all I fear that the nature of knowledge, which is the main subject of our discussion, may be thrust out of sight by the unbidden guests who will come pouring in upon our feast of discourse, if we let them in—besides, the question which is now stirring is of immense extent, and will be treated unfairly if only considered by the way; or

if treated adequately and at length, will put into the shade the other
question of knowledge. Neither the one nor the other can be allowed;
b but I must try by my art of midwifery to deliver Theaetetus of his
conceptions about knowledge.

THEAETETUS: Very well; do so if you will.

SOCRATES: Then now, Theaetetus, take another view of the subject: you answered that knowledge is perception?

THEAETETUS: I did.

SOCRATES: And if anyone were to ask you: With what does a man see black and white colors? And with what does he hear high and low sounds? You would say, if I am not mistaken, "With the eyes and with the ears."

THEAETETUS: I should.

c *SOCRATES*: The free use of words and phrases, rather than minute precision, is generally characteristic of a liberal education, and the opposite is pedantic; but sometimes precision is necessary, and I believe that the answer which you have just given is open to the charge of incorrectness; for which is more correct, to say that we see or hear with the eyes and with the ears, or through the eyes and through the ears.

THEAETETUS: I should say "through," Socrates, rather than "with."

d *SOCRATES*: Yes, my boy, for no one can suppose that in each of us, as in a sort of Trojan horse, there are perched a number of unconnected senses, which do not all meet in some one nature, the mind, or whatever we please to call it, of which they are the instruments, and with which through them we perceive objects of sense.

THEAETETUS: I agree with you in that opinion.

SOCRATES: The reason why I am thus precise is, because I want to know
e whether, when we perceive black and white through the eyes, and
again, other qualities through other organs, we do not perceive them
with one and the same part of ourselves, and, if you were asked, you
might refer all such perceptions to the body. Perhaps, however, I had
better allow you to answer for yourself and not interfere. Tell me,
then, are not the organs through which you perceive warm and hard
and light and sweet, organs of the body?

THEAETETUS: Of the body, certainly.

SOCRATES: And you would admit that what you perceive through one fac-
185a ulty you cannot perceive through another; the objects of hearing, for
example, cannot be perceived through sight, or the objects of sight
through hearing?

THEAETETUS: Of course not.

Socrates: If you have any thought about both of them, this common perception cannot come to you, either through the one or the other organ?

Theaetetus: It cannot.

Socrates: How about sounds and colors: in the first place you would admit that they both exist?

Theaetetus: Yes.

Socrates: And that either of them is different from the other, and the same with itself?

Theaetetus: Certainly. b

Socrates: And that both are two and each of them one?

Theaetetus: Yes.

Socrates: You can further observe whether they are like or unlike one another?

Theaetetus: I dare say.

Socrates: But through what do you perceive all this about them? For neither through hearing nor yet through seeing can you apprehend that which they have in common. Let me give you an illustration of the point at issue: If there were any meaning in asking whether sounds
and colors are saline or not, you would be able to tell me what faculty c
would consider the question. It would not be sight or hearing, but some other.

Theaetetus: Certainly; the faculty of taste.

Socrates: Very good; and now tell me what is the power which discerns, not only in sensible objects, but in all things, universal notions, such as those which are called being and not-being, and those others about which we were just asking—what organs will you assign for the perception of these notions?

Theaetetus: You are thinking of being and not being, likeness and unlikeness, sameness and difference, and also of unity and other numbers d
which are applied to objects of sense; and you mean to ask, through what bodily organ the soul perceives odd and even numbers and other arithmetical conceptions.

Socrates: You follow me excellently, Theaetetus; that is precisely what I am asking.

Theaetetus: Indeed, Socrates, I cannot answer; my only notion is, that these, unlike objects of sense, have no separate organ, but that the mind, by
a power of her own, contemplates the universals in all things. e

Socrates: You are a beauty, Theaetetus, and not ugly, as Theodorus was saying; for he who utters the beautiful is himself beautiful and good.

And besides being beautiful, you have done me a kindness in releasing me from a very long discussion, if you are clear that the soul views some things by herself and others through the bodily organs. For that was my own opinion, and I wanted you to agree with me.

186a *THEAETETUS*: I am quite clear.

SOCRATES: And to which class would you refer being or essence; for this, of all our notions, is the most universal?

THEAETETUS: I should say, to that class which the soul aspires to know of herself.

SOCRATES: And would you say this also of like and unlike, same and other?

THEAETETUS: Yes.

SOCRATES: And would you say the same of the noble and base, and of good and evil?

THEAETETUS: These I conceive to be notions which are essentially relative, and which the soul also perceives by comparing in herself
b things past and present with the future.

SOCRATES: And does she not perceive the hardness of that which is hard by the touch, and the softness of that which is soft equally by the touch?

THEAETETUS: Yes.

SOCRATES: But their essence and what they are, and their opposition to one another, and the essential nature of this opposition, the soul herself endeavors to decide for us by the review and comparison of them?

THEAETETUS: Certainly.

c *SOCRATES*: The simple sensations which reach the soul through the body are given at birth to men and animals by nature, but their reflections on the being and use of them are slowly and hardly gained, if they are ever gained, by education and long experience.

THEAETETUS: Assuredly.

SOCRATES: And can a man attain truth who fails of attaining being?

THEAETETUS: Impossible.

SOCRATES: And can he who misses the truth of anything, have a knowledge of that thing?

d *THEAETETUS*: He cannot.

SOCRATES: Then knowledge does not consist in impressions of sense, but in reasoning about them; in that only, and not in the mere impression, truth and being can be attained?

THEAETETUS: Clearly.

SOCRATES: And would you call the two processes by the same name, when there is so great a difference between them?

THEAETETUS: That would certainly not be right.

SOCRATES: And what name would you give to seeing, hearing, smelling, being cold and being hot?

THEAETETUS: I should call all of them perceiving—what other name could e
be given to them?

SOCRATES: Perception would be the collective name of them?

THEAETETUS: Certainly.

SOCRATES: Which, as we say, has no part in the attainment of truth any more than of being?

THEAETETUS: Certainly not.

SOCRATES: And therefore not in science or knowledge?

THEAETETUS: No.

SOCRATES: Then perception, Theaetetus, can never be the same as knowledge or science?

THEAETETUS: Clearly not, Socrates; and knowledge has now been most distinctly proved to be different from perception.

SOCRATES: But the original aim of our discussion was to find out rather 187a
what knowledge is than what it is not; at the same time we have made some progress, for we no longer seek for knowledge in perception at all, but in that other process, however called, in which the mind is alone and engaged with being.

THEAETETUS: You mean, Socrates, if I am not mistaken, what is called thinking or opining.

SOCRATES: You conceive truly. And now, my friend, please to begin again b
at this point; and having wiped out of your memory all that has preceded, see if you have arrived at any clearer view, and once more say what is knowledge.

THEAETETUS: I cannot say, Socrates, that all opinion is knowledge, because there may be a false opinion; but I will venture to assert, that knowledge is true opinion: let this then be my reply; and if this is hereafter disproved, I must try to find another.

SOCRATES: That is the way in which you ought to answer, Theaetetus, and
not in your former hesitating strain, for if we are bold we shall gain
one of two advantages; either we shall find what we seek, or we shall be c
less likely to think that we know what we do not know—in either case we shall be richly rewarded. And now, what are you saying? Are there two sorts of opinion, one true and the other false; and do you define knowledge to be the true?

THEAETETUS: Yes, according to my present view.

SOCRATES: Is it still worth our while to resume the discussion touching opinion?

THEAETETUS: To what are you alluding?

d *SOCRATES*: There is a point which often troubles me, and is a great perplexity to me, both in regard to myself and others. I cannot make out the nature or origin of the mental experience to which I refer.

THEAETETUS: Pray what is it?

SOCRATES: How there can be false opinion—that difficulty still troubles the eye of my mind; and I am uncertain whether I shall leave the question, or begin over again in a new way.

THEAETETUS: Begin again, Socrates—at least if you think that there is the slightest necessity for doing so. Were not you and Theodorus just now remarking very truly, that in discussions of this kind we may take our own time?

e *SOCRATES*: You are quite right, and perhaps there will be no harm in retracing our steps and beginning again. Better a little which is well done, than a great deal imperfectly.

THEAETETUS: Certainly.

SOCRATES: Well, and what is the difficulty? Do we not speak of false opinion, and say that one man holds a false and another a true opinion, as though there were some natural distinction between them?

THEAETETUS: We certainly say so.

188a *SOCRATES*: All things and everything are either known or not known. I leave out of view the intermediate conceptions of learning and forgetting, because they have nothing to do with our present question.

THEAETETUS: There can be no doubt, Socrates, if you exclude these, that there is no other alternative but knowing or not knowing a thing.

SOCRATES: That point being now determined, must we not say that he who has an opinion, must have an opinion about something which he knows or does not know?

THEAETETUS: He must.

b *SOCRATES*: He who knows, cannot but know; and he who does not know, cannot know?

THEAETETUS: Of course.

SOCRATES: What shall we say then? When a man has a false opinion does he think that which he knows to be some other thing which he knows, and knowing both, is he at the same time ignorant of both?

THEAETETUS: That, Socrates, is impossible.

Socrates: But perhaps he thinks of something which he does not know as some other thing which he does not know; for example, he knows neither Theaetetus nor Socrates, and yet he fancies that Theaetetus is Socrates, or Socrates Theaetetus?

Theaetetus: How can he? c

Socrates: But surely he cannot suppose what he knows to be what he does not know, or what he does not know to be what he knows?

Theaetetus: That would be monstrous.

Socrates: Where, then, is false opinion? For if all things are either known or unknown, there can be no opinion which is not comprehended under this alternative, and so false opinion is excluded.

Theaetetus: Most true.

Socrates: Suppose that we remove the question out of the sphere of knowing or not knowing, into that of being and not-being. d

Theaetetus: What do you mean?

Socrates: May we not suspect the simple truth to be that he who thinks about anything, that which is not, will necessarily think what is false, whatever in other respects may be the state of his mind?

Theaetetus: That, again, is not unlikely, Socrates.

Socrates: Then suppose some one to say to us, Theaetetus: Is it possible for any man to think that which is not, either as a self-existent substance or as a predicate of something else? And suppose that we answer, "Yes, he
can, when he thinks what is not true." That will be our answer? e

Theaetetus: Yes.

Socrates: But is there any parallel to this?

Theaetetus: What do you mean?

Socrates: Can a man see something and yet see nothing?

Theaetetus: Impossible.

Socrates: But if he sees any one thing, he sees something that exists. Do you suppose that what is one is ever to be found among non-existing things?

Theaetetus: I do not.

Socrates: He then who sees some one thing, sees something which is?

Theaetetus: Clearly.

Socrates: And he who hears anything, hears some one thing, and hears 189a
that which is?

Theaetetus: Yes.

Socrates: And he who touches anything, touches something which is one and therefore is?

THEAETETUS: That again is true.

SOCRATES: And does not he who thinks, think some one thing?

THEAETETUS: Certainly.

SOCRATES: And does not he who thinks some one thing, think something which is?

THEAETETUS: I agree.

SOCRATES: Then he who thinks of that which is not, thinks of nothing?

THEAETETUS: Clearly.

SOCRATES: And he who thinks of nothing, does not think at all?

THEAETETUS: Obviously.

b *SOCRATES*: Then no one can think that which is not, either as a self-existent substance or as a predicate of something else?

THEAETETUS: Clearly not.

SOCRATES: Then to think falsely is different from thinking that which is not?

THEAETETUS: It would seem so.

SOCRATES: Then false opinion has no existence in us, either in the sphere of being or of knowledge?

THEAETETUS: Certainly not.

SOCRATES: But may not the following be the description of what we express by this name?

THEAETETUS: What?

c *SOCRATES*: May we not suppose that false opinion or thought is a sort of heterodoxy; a person may make an exchange in his mind, and say that one real object is another real object. For thus he always thinks that which is, but he puts one thing in place of another; and missing the aim of his thoughts, he may be truly said to have false opinion.

THEAETETUS: Now you appear to me to have spoken the exact truth: when a man puts the base in the place of the noble, or the noble in the place of the base, then he has truly false opinion.

SOCRATES: I see, Theaetetus, that your fear has disappeared, and that you are beginning to despise me.

THEAETETUS: What makes you say so?

d *SOCRATES*: You think, if I am not mistaken, that your "truly false" is safe from censure, and that I shall never ask whether there can be a swift which is slow, or a heavy which is light, or any other self-contradictory thing, which works, not according to its own nature, but according to that of its opposite. But I will not insist upon this, for I do not wish needlessly to discourage you. And so you are satisfied that false opinion is heterodoxy, or the thought of something else?

Theaetetus: I am.

Socrates: It is possible then upon your view for the mind to conceive of one thing as another?

Theaetetus: True.

Socrates: But must not the mind, or thinking power, which misplaces e
them, have a conception either of both objects or of one of them?

Theaetetus: Certainly.

Socrates: Either together or in succession?

Theaetetus: Very good.

Socrates: And do you mean by conceiving, the same which I mean?

Theaetetus: What is that?

Socrates: I mean the conversation which the soul holds with herself in considering of anything. I speak of what I scarcely understand; but
the soul when thinking appears to me to be just talking—asking ques- 190a
tions of herself and answering them, affirming and denying. And when she has arrived at a decision, either gradually or by a sudden impulse, and has at last agreed, and does not doubt, this is called her opinion. I say, then, that to form an opinion is to speak, and opinion is a word spoken—I mean, to oneself and in silence, not aloud or to another: What think you?

Theaetetus: I agree.

Socrates: Then when anyone thinks of one thing as another, he is saying to himself that one thing is another?

Theaetetus: Yes. b

Socrates: But do you ever remember saying to yourself that the noble is certainly base, or the unjust just; or, best of all—have you ever attempted to convince yourself that one thing is another? Nay, not even in sleep, did you ever venture to say to yourself that odd is even, or anything of the kind?

Theaetetus: Never.

Socrates: And do you suppose that any other man, either in his senses or c
out of them, ever seriously tried to persuade himself that an ox is a horse, or that two are one?

Theaetetus: Certainly not.

Socrates: But if thinking is talking to oneself, no one speaking and thinking of two objects, and apprehending them both in his soul, will say and think that the one is the other of them, and I must add, that even you, lover of dispute as you are, had better let the word "other" alone (i.e., not insist that "one" and "other" are the same

(Both words in Greek are called eteron: compare Parmen.; Euthyd.)).
d I mean to say, that no one thinks the noble to be base, or anything of the kind.

THEAETETUS: I will give up the word "other," Socrates; and I agree to what you say.

SOCRATES: If a man has both of them in his thoughts, he cannot think that the one of them is the other?

THEAETETUS: True.

SOCRATES: Neither, if he has one of them only in his mind and not the other, can he think that one is the other?

THEAETETUS: True; for we should have to suppose that he apprehends that which is not in his thoughts at all.

e *SOCRATES*: Then no one who has either both or only one of the two objects in his mind can think that the one is the other. And therefore, he who maintains that false opinion is heterodoxy is talking nonsense; for neither in this, any more than in the previous way, can false opinion exist in us.

THEAETETUS: No.

SOCRATES: But if, Theaetetus, this is not admitted, we shall be driven into many absurdities.

THEAETETUS: What are they?

SOCRATES: I will not tell you until I have endeavored to consider the matter
191a from every point of view. For I should be ashamed of us if we were driven in our perplexity to admit the absurd consequences of which I speak. But if we find the solution, and get away from them, we may regard them only as the difficulties of others, and the ridicule will not attach to us. On the other hand, if we utterly fail, I suppose that we must be humble, and allow the argument to trample us under foot, as the sea-sick passenger is trampled upon by the sailor, and to do anything to us. Listen, then, while I tell you how I hope to find a way out of our difficulty.

THEAETETUS: Let me hear.

SOCRATES: I think that we were wrong in denying that a man could think
b what he knew to be what he did not know; and that there is a way in which such a deception is possible.

THEAETETUS: You mean to say, as I suspected at the time, that I may know Socrates, and at a distance see some one who is unknown to me, and whom I mistake for him—then the deception will occur?

SOCRATES: But has not that position been relinquished by us, because involving the absurdity that we should know and not know the things which we know?

THEAETETUS: True.

SOCRATES: Let us make the assertion in another form, which may or may not have a favorable issue; but as we are in a great strait, every argument should be turned over and tested. Tell me, then, whether I am right in saying that you may learn a thing which at one time you did not know? c

THEAETETUS: Certainly you may.

SOCRATES: And another and another?

THEAETETUS: Yes.

SOCRATES: I would have you imagine, then, that there exists in the mind of man a block of wax, which is of different sizes in different men; harder, moister, and having more or less of purity in one than another, and in d
some of an intermediate quality.

THEAETETUS: I see.

SOCRATES: Let us say that this tablet is a gift of Memory, the mother of the Muses; and that when we wish to remember anything which we have seen, or heard, or thought in our own minds, we hold the wax to the perceptions and thoughts, and in that material receive the impression of them as from the seal of a ring; and that we remember and know what is imprinted as long as the image lasts; but when the image is effaced, or cannot be taken, then we forget and do not know. e

THEAETETUS: Very good.

SOCRATES: Now, when a person has this knowledge, and is considering something which he sees or hears, may not false opinion arise in the following manner?

THEAETETUS: In what manner?

SOCRATES: When he thinks what he knows, sometimes to be what he knows, and sometimes to be what he does not know. We were wrong before in denying the possibility of this.

THEAETETUS: And how would you amend the former statement?

SOCRATES: I should begin by making a list of the impossible cases which 192a
must be excluded. (1) No one can think one thing to be another when he does not perceive either of them, but has the memorial or seal of both of them in his mind; nor can any mistaking of one thing for another occur, when he only knows one, and does not know, and

has no impression of the other; nor can he think that one thing which
he does not know is another thing which he does not know, or that
b what he does not know is what he knows; nor (2) that one thing which
he perceives is another thing which he perceives, or that something
which he perceives is something which he does not perceive; or that
something which he does not perceive is something else which he
does not perceive; or that something which he does not perceive is
something which he perceives; nor again (3) can he think that something which he knows and perceives, and of which he has the
impression coinciding with sense, is something else which he knows
and perceives, and of which he has the impression coinciding with
sense; this last case, if possible, is still more inconceivable than the
c others; nor (4) can he think that something which he knows and
perceives, and of which he has the memorial coinciding with sense, is
something else which he knows; nor so long as these agree, can he
think that a thing which he knows and perceives is another thing
which he perceives; or that a thing which he does not know and does
not perceive, is the same as another thing which he does not know
and does not perceive; nor again, can he suppose that a thing which
he does not know and does not perceive is the same as another thing
which he does not know; or that a thing which he does not know and
does not perceive is another thing which he does not perceive: All
these utterly and absolutely exclude the possibility of false opinion.
The only cases, if any, which remain, are the following.

THEAETETUS: What are they? If you tell me, I may perhaps understand you better; but at present I am unable to follow you.

SOCRATES: A person may think that some things which he knows, or which
he perceives and does not know, are some other things which he
d knows and perceives; or that some things which he knows and perceives, are other things which he knows and perceives.

THEAETETUS: I understand you less than ever now.

SOCRATES: Hear me once more, then: I, knowing Theodorus, and remembering in my own mind what sort of person he is, and also what sort of person Theaetetus is, at one time see them, and at another time do not see them, and sometimes I touch them, and at another time not, or at one time I may hear them or perceive them in some other way, and at another time not perceive them, but still I remember them, and know them in my own mind.

e *THEAETETUS*: Very true.

Socrates: Then, first of all, I want you to understand that a man may or may not perceive sensibly that which he knows.

Theaetetus: True.

Socrates: And that which he does not know will sometimes not be perceived by him and sometimes will be perceived and only perceived?

Theaetetus: That is also true.

Socrates: See whether you can follow me better now: Socrates can recognize
Theodorus and Theaetetus, but he sees neither of them, nor does he 193a
perceive them in any other way; he cannot then by any possibility imagine in his own mind that Theaetetus is Theodorus. Am I not right?

Theaetetus: You are quite right.

Socrates: Then that was the first case of which I spoke.

Theaetetus: Yes.

Socrates: The second case was, that I, knowing one of you and not knowing the other, and perceiving neither, can never think him whom I know to be him whom I do not know.

Theaetetus: True.

Socrates: In the third case, not knowing and not perceiving either of b
you, I cannot think that one of you whom I do not know is the other whom I do not know. I need not again go over the catalogue of excluded cases, in which I cannot form a false opinion about you and Theodorus, either when I know both or when I am in ignorance of both, or when I know one and not the other. And the same of perceiving: do you understand me?

Theaetetus: I do.

Socrates: The only possibility of erroneous opinion is, when knowing you
and Theodorus, and having on the waxen block the impression of c
both of you given as by a seal, but seeing you imperfectly and at a distance, I try to assign the right impression of memory to the right visual impression, and to fit this into its own print: if I succeed, recognition will take place; but if I fail and transpose them, putting the foot into the wrong shoe—that is to say, putting the vision of either of you on to the wrong impression, or if my mind, like the sight in a mirror,
which is transferred from right to left, err by reason of some similar d
affection, then "heterodoxy" and false opinion ensues.

Theaetetus: Yes, Socrates, you have described the nature of opinion with wonderful exactness.

Socrates: Or again, when I know both of you, and perceive as well as know one of you, but not the other, and my knowledge of him does not accord with perception—that was the case put by me just now which you did not understand.

THEAETETUS: No, I did not.

SOCRATES: I meant to say, that when a person knows and perceives one of
e you, his knowledge coincides with his perception, he will never think him to be some other person, whom he knows and perceives, and the knowledge of whom coincides with his perception—for that also was a case supposed.

THEAETETUS: True.

SOCRATES: But there was an omission of the further case, in which, as we
194a now say, false opinion may arise, when knowing both, and seeing, or having some other sensible perception of both, I fail in holding the seal over against the corresponding sensation; like a bad archer, I miss and fall wide of the mark—and this is called falsehood.

THEAETETUS: Yes; it is rightly so called.

SOCRATES: When, therefore, perception is present to one of the seals or impressions but not to the other, and the mind fits the seal of the absent perception on the one which is present, in any case of this sort
b the mind is deceived; in a word, if our view is sound, there can be no error or deception about things which a man does not know and has never perceived, but only in things which are known and perceived; in these alone opinion turns and twists about, and becomes alternately true and false; true when the seals and impressions of sense meet straight and opposite—false when they go awry and crooked.

THEAETETUS: And is not that, Socrates, nobly said?

c *SOCRATES*: Nobly! Yes; but wait a little and hear the explanation, and then you will say so with more reason; for to think truly is noble and to be deceived is base.

THEAETETUS: Undoubtedly.

SOCRATES: And the origin of truth and error is as follows: When the wax in the soul of anyone is deep and abundant, and smooth and perfectly tempered, then the impressions which pass through the senses and sink into the heart of the soul, as Homer says in a parable, meaning to indicate the likeness of the soul to wax (Kerh Kerhos); these, I say,
d being pure and clear, and having a sufficient depth of wax, are also lasting, and minds, such as these, easily learn and easily retain, and are not liable to confusion, but have true thoughts, for they have plenty of room, and having clear impressions of things, as we term them, quickly

distribute them into their proper places on the block. And such men are called wise. Do you agree?

Theaetetus: Entirely.

Socrates: But when the heart of anyone is shaggy—a quality which the e
all-wise poet commends, or muddy and of impure wax, or very soft, or
very hard, then there is a corresponding defect in the mind—the soft
are good at learning, but apt to forget; and the hard are the reverse;
the shaggy and rugged and gritty, or those who have an admixture of
earth or dung in their composition, have the impressions indistinct,
as also the hard, for there is no depth in them; and the soft too are 195a
indistinct, for their impressions are easily confused and effaced. Yet greater is the indistinctness when they are all jostled together in a little soul, which has no room. These are the natures which have false opinion; for when they see or hear or think of anything, they are slow in assigning the right objects to the right impressions—in their stupidity they contuse them, and are apt to see and hear and think amiss—and such men are said to be deceived in their knowledge of objects, and ignorant.

Theaetetus: No man, Socrates, can say anything truer than that. b

Socrates: Then now we may admit the existence of false opinion in us?

Theaetetus: Certainly.

Socrates: And of true opinion also?

Theaetetus: Yes.

Socrates: We have at length satisfactorily proven beyond a doubt there are these two sorts of opinion?

Theaetetus: Undoubtedly.

Socrates: Alas, Theaetetus, what a tiresome creature is a man who is fond of talking!

Theaetetus: What makes you say so?

Socrates: Because I am disheartened at my own stupidity and tiresome c
garrulity; for what other term will describe the habit of a man who is always arguing on all sides of a question; whose dulness cannot be convinced, and who will never leave off?

Theaetetus: But what puts you out of heart?

Socrates: I am not only out of heart, but in positive despair; for I do not know what to answer if anyone were to ask me: O Socrates, have you indeed discovered that false opinion arises neither in the comparison of perceptions with one another nor yet in thought, but in union of d thought and perception? Yes, I shall say, with the complacence of one who thinks that he has made a noble discovery.

THEAETETUS: I see no reason why we should be ashamed of our demonstration, Socrates.

SOCRATES: He will say: You mean to argue that the man whom we only think of and do not see, cannot be confused with the horse which we do not see or touch, but only think of and do not perceive? That I believe to be my meaning, I shall reply.

THEAETETUS: Quite right.

e *SOCRATES*: Well, then, he will say, according to that argument, the number eleven, which is only thought, can never be mistaken for twelve, which is only thought: How would you answer him?

THEAETETUS: I should say that a mistake may very likely arise between the eleven or twelve which are seen or handled, but that no similar mistake can arise between the eleven and twelve which are in the mind.

SOCRATES: Well, but do you think that no one ever put before his own
196a mind five and seven—I do not mean five or seven men or horses, but five or seven in the abstract, which, as we say, are recorded on the waxen block, and in which false opinion is held to be impossible; did no man ever ask himself how many these numbers make when added together, and answer that they are eleven, while another thinks that they are twelve, or would all agree in thinking and saying that they are twelve?

b *THEAETETUS*: Certainly not; many would think that they are eleven, and in the higher numbers the chance of error is greater still; for I assume you to be speaking of numbers in general.

SOCRATES: Exactly; and I want you to consider whether this does not imply that the twelve in the waxen block are supposed to be eleven?

THEAETETUS: Yes, that seems to be the case.

SOCRATES: Then do we not come back to the old difficulty? For he who makes such a mistake does think one thing which he knows to be another thing which he knows; but this, as we said, was impossible, and afforded an irresistible proof of the nonexistence of false opinion,
c because otherwise the same person would inevitably know and not know the same thing at the same time.

THEAETETUS: Most true.

SOCRATES: Then false opinion cannot be explained as a confusion of thought and sense, for in that case we could not have been mistaken about pure conceptions of thought; and thus we are obliged to say, either that false opinion does not exist, or that a man may not know that which he knows; which alternative do you prefer?

THEAETETUS: It is hard to determine, Socrates.

SOCRATES: And yet the argument will scarcely admit of both. But, as we are d
at our wits' end, suppose that we do a shameless thing?

THEAETETUS: What is it?

SOCRATES: Let us attempt to explain the verb "to know."

THEAETETUS: And why should that be shameless?

SOCRATES: You seem not to be aware that the whole of our discussion from the very beginning has been a search after knowledge, of which we are assumed not to know the nature.

THEAETETUS: Nay, but I am well aware.

SOCRATES: And is it not shameless when we do not know what knowledge is, to be explaining the verb "to know"? The truth is, Theaetetus, that we
have long been infected with logical impurity. Thousands of times have e
we repeated the words "we know," and "do not know," and "we have or have not science or knowledge," as if we could understand what we are saying to one another, so long as we remain ignorant about knowledge; and at this moment we are using the words "we understand," "we are ignorant," as though we could still employ them when deprived of knowledge or science.

THEAETETUS: But if you avoid these expressions, Socrates, how will you ever argue at all?

SOCRATES: I could not, being the man I am. The case would be different 197a
if I were a true hero of dialectic: and O that such an one were present! For he would have told us to avoid the use of these terms; at the same time he would not have spared in you and me the faults which I have noted. But, seeing that we are no great wits, shall I venture to say what knowing is? For I think that the attempt may be worth making.

THEAETETUS: Then by all means venture, and no one shall find fault with you for using the forbidden terms.

SOCRATES: You have heard the common explanation of the verb "to know"?

THEAETETUS: I think so, but I do not remember it at the moment.

SOCRATES: They explain the word "to know" as meaning "to have knowledge." b

THEAETETUS: True.

SOCRATES: I should like to make a slight change, and say "to possess" knowledge.

THEAETETUS: How do the two expressions differ?

SOCRATES: Perhaps there may be no difference; but still I should like you to hear my view, that you may help me to test it.

THEAETETUS: I will, if I can.

SOCRATES: I should distinguish "having" from "possessing": for example, a man may buy and keep under his control a garment which he does not wear; and then we should say, not that he has, but that he possesses the garment.

THEAETETUS: It would be the correct expression.

c *SOCRATES*: Well, may not a man "possess" and yet not "have" knowledge in the sense of which I am speaking? As you may suppose a man to have caught wild birds—doves or any other birds—and to be keeping them in an aviary which he has constructed at home; we might say of him in one sense, that he always has them because he possesses them, might we not?

THEAETETUS: Yes.

SOCRATES: And yet, in another sense, he has none of them; but they are in his power, and he has got them under his hand in an enclosure of his
d own, and can take and have them whenever he likes; he can catch any which he likes, and let the bird go again, and he may do so as often as he pleases.

THEAETETUS: True.

SOCRATES: Once more, then, as in what preceded we made a sort of waxen figment in the mind, so let us now suppose that in the mind of each man there is an aviary of all sorts of birds—some flocking together apart from the rest, others in small groups, others solitary, flying anywhere and everywhere.

e *THEAETETUS*: Let us imagine such an aviary—and what is to follow?

SOCRATES: We may suppose that the birds are kinds of knowledge, and that when we were children, this receptacle was empty; whenever a man has gotten and detained in the enclosure a kind of knowledge, he may be said to have learned or discovered the thing which is the subject of the knowledge: and this is to know.

THEAETETUS: Granted.

198a *SOCRATES*: And further, when anyone wishes to catch any of these knowledges or sciences, and having taken, to hold it, and again to let them go, how will he express himself? Will he describe the "catching" of them and the original "possession" in the same words? I will make my meaning clearer by an example: You admit that there is an art of arithmetic?

THEAETETUS: To be sure.

SOCRATES: Conceive this under the form of a hunt after the science of odd and even in general.

THEAETETUS: I follow.

SOCRATES: Having the use of the art, the arithmetician, if I am not mistaken, has the conceptions of number under his hand, and can b
transmit them to another.

THEAETETUS: Yes.

SOCRATES: And when transmitting them he may be said to teach them, and when receiving to learn them, and when receiving to learn them, and when having them in possession in the aforesaid aviary he may be said to know them.

THEAETETUS: Exactly.

SOCRATES: Attend to what follows: must not the perfect arithmetician know all numbers, for he has the science of all numbers in his mind?

THEAETETUS: True.

SOCRATES: And he can reckon abstract numbers in his head, or things c
about him which are numerable?

THEAETETUS: Of course he can.

SOCRATES: And to reckon is simply to consider how much such and such a number amounts to?

THEAETETUS: Very true.

SOCRATES: And so he appears to be searching into something which he knows, as if he did not know it, for we have already admitted that he knows all numbers; you have heard these perplexing questions raised?

THEAETETUS: I have.

SOCRATES: May we not pursue the image of the doves, and say that the chase d
after knowledge is of two kinds? One kind is prior to possession and for the sake of possession, and the other for the sake of taking and holding in the hands that which is possessed already. And thus, when a man has learned and known something long ago, he may resume and get hold of the knowledge which he has long possessed, but has not at hand in his mind.

THEAETETUS: True.

SOCRATES: That was my reason for asking how we ought to speak when an e
arithmetician sets about numbering, or a grammarian about reading? Shall we say, that although he knows, he comes back to himself to learn what he already knows?

THEAETETUS: It would be too absurd, Socrates.

199a *SOCRATES*: Shall we say then that he is going to read or number what he does not know, although we have admitted that he knows all letters and all numbers?

THEAETETUS: That, again, would be an absurdity.

SOCRATES: Then shall we say that about names we care nothing? Anyone
may twist and turn the words "knowing" and "learning" in any way
which he likes, but since we have determined that the possession of
b knowledge is not the having or using it, we do assert that a man cannot not possess that which he possesses; and, therefore, in no case
can a man not know that which he knows, but he may get a false
opinion about it; for he may have the knowledge, not of this particular thing, but of some other; when the various numbers and forms
of knowledge are flying about in the aviary, and wishing to capture
a certain sort of knowledge out of the general store, he takes the
wrong one by mistake, that is to say, when he thought eleven to be
twelve, he got hold of the ring-dove which he had in his mind, when
he wanted the pigeon.

THEAETETUS: A very rational explanation.

SOCRATES: But when he catches the one which he wants, then he is not
c deceived, and has an opinion of what is, and thus false and true opinion
may exist, and the difficulties which were previously raised disappear.
I dare say that you agree with me, do you not?

THEAETETUS: Yes.

SOCRATES: And so we are rid of the difficulty of a man's not knowing what he knows, for we are not driven to the inference that he does not possess what he possesses, whether he be or be not deceived. And yet I fear that a greater difficulty is looking in at the window.

THEAETETUS: What is it?

SOCRATES: How can the exchange of one knowledge for another ever become false opinion?

THEAETETUS: What do you mean?

d *SOCRATES*: In the first place, how can a man who has the knowledge of anything be ignorant of that which he knows, not by reason of ignorance, but by reason of his own knowledge? And, again, is it not an extreme absurdity that he should suppose another thing to be this, and this to be another thing; that, having knowledge present with him in his mind, he should still know nothing and be ignorant of all things? You might as well argue that ignorance may make a man know, and blindness make him see, as that knowledge can make him ignorant.

THEAETETUS: Perhaps, Socrates, we may have been wrong in making only e
forms of knowledge our birds: whereas there ought to have been forms
of ignorance as well, flying about together in the mind, and then he
who sought to take one of them might sometimes catch a form of
knowledge, and sometimes a form of ignorance; and thus he would
have a false opinion from ignorance, but a true one from knowledge,
about the same thing.

SOCRATES: I cannot help praising you, Theaetetus, and yet I must beg you to
reconsider your words. Let us grant what you say—then, according
to you, he who takes ignorance will have a false opinion—am I right? 200a

THEAETETUS: Yes.

SOCRATES: He will certainly not think that he has a false opinion?

THEAETETUS: Of course not.

SOCRATES: He will think that his opinion is true, and he will fancy that he knows the things about which he has been deceived?

THEAETETUS: Certainly.

SOCRATES: Then he will think that he has captured knowledge and not ignorance?

THEAETETUS: Clearly.

SOCRATES: And thus, after going a long way round, we are once more face
to face with our original difficulty. The hero of dialectic will retort
upon us: "O my excellent friends, he will say, laughing, if a man knows
the form of ignorance and the form of knowledge, can he think that b
one of them which he knows is the other which he knows? Or, if he
knows neither of them, can he think that the one which he knows not
is another which he knows not? Or, if he knows one and not the
other, can he think the one which he knows to be the one which he
does not know? Or the one which he does not know to be the one
which he knows? Or will you tell me that there are other forms of
knowledge which distinguish the right and wrong birds, and which
the owner keeps in some other aviaries or graven on waxen blocks c
according to your foolish images, and which he may be said to know
while he possesses them, even though he have them not at hand in his
mind? And thus, in a perpetual circle, you will be compelled to go
round and round, and you will make no progress." What are we to say
in reply, Theaetetus?

THEAETETUS: Indeed, Socrates, I do not know what we are to say.

SOCRATES: Are not his reproaches just, and does not the argument truly show that we are wrong in seeking for false opinion until we know d what knowledge is; that must be first ascertained; then, the nature of false opinion?

THEAETETUS: I cannot but agree with you, Socrates, so far as we have yet gone.

SOCRATES: Then, once more, what shall we say that knowledge is? For we are not going to lose heart as yet.

THEAETETUS: Certainly, I shall not lose heart, if you do not.

SOCRATES: What definition will be most consistent with our former views?

e *THEAETETUS*: I cannot think of any but our old one, Socrates.

SOCRATES: What was it?

THEAETETUS: Knowledge was said by us to be true opinion; and true opinion is surely unerring, and the results which follow from it are all noble and good.

SOCRATES: He who led the way into the river, Theaetetus, said "The experiment will show"; and perhaps if we go forward in the search, we may
201a stumble upon the thing which we are looking for; but if we stay where we are, nothing will come to light.

THEAETETUS: Very true; let us go forward and try.

SOCRATES: The trail soon comes to an end, for a whole profession is against us.

THEAETETUS: How is that, and what profession do you mean?

SOCRATES: The profession of the great wise ones who are called orators and lawyers; for these persuade men by their art and make them think whatever they like, but they do not teach them. Do you imagine that
b there are any teachers in the world so clever as to be able to convince others of the truth about acts of robbery or violence, of which they were not eyewitnesses, while a little water is flowing in the clepsydra?

THEAETETUS: Certainly not, they can only persuade them.

SOCRATES: And would you not say that persuading them is making them have an opinion?

THEAETETUS: To be sure.

SOCRATES: When, therefore, judges are justly persuaded about matters which you can know only by seeing them, and not in any other way, and when thus judging of them from report they attain a true opinion
c about them, they judge without knowledge, and yet are rightly persuaded, if they have judged well.

THEAETETUS: Certainly.

SOCRATES: And yet, O my friend, if true opinion in law courts and knowledge are the same, the perfect judge could not have judged rightly without knowledge; and therefore I must infer that they are not the same.

THEAETETUS: That is a distinction, Socrates, which I have heard made by
some one else, but I had forgotten it. He said that true opinion, com- d
bined with reason, was knowledge, but that the opinion which had no
reason was out of the sphere of knowledge; and that things of which
there is no rational account are not knowable—such was the singular
expression which he used—and that things which have a reason or
explanation are knowable.

SOCRATES: Excellent; but then, how did he distinguish between things
which are and are not "knowable"? I wish that you would repeat to
me what he said, and then I shall know whether you and I have heard
the same tale.

THEAETETUS: I do not know whether I can recall it; but if another person
would tell me, I think that I could follow him.

SOCRATES: Let me give you, then, a dream in return for a dream:
Methought that I too had a dream, and I heard in my dream that the e
primeval letters or elements out of which you and I and all other
things are compounded, have no reason or explanation; you can only
name them, but no predicate can be either affirmed or denied of
them, for in the one case existence, in the other nonexistence is 202a
already implied, neither of which must be added, if you mean to
speak of this or that thing by itself alone. It should not be called itself,
or that, or each, or alone, or this, or the like; for these go about everywhere and are applied to all things, but are distinct from them;
whereas, if the first elements could be described, and had a definition
of their own, they would be spoken of apart from all else. But none of
these primeval elements can be defined; they can only be named, for b
they have nothing but a name, and the things which are compounded
of them, as they are complex, are expressed by a combination of
names, for the combination of names is the essence of a definition.
Thus, then, the elements or letters are only objects of perception, and
cannot be defined or known; but the syllables or combinations of
them are known and expressed, and are apprehended by true opinion. When, therefore, anyone forms the true opinion of anything
without rational explanation, you may say that his mind is truly exer- c
cised, but has no knowledge; for he who cannot give and receive a
reason for a thing, has no knowledge of that thing; but when he adds
rational explanation, then, he is perfected in knowledge and may be
all that I have been denying of him. Was that the form in which the
dream appeared to you?

THEAETETUS: Precisely.

SOCRATES: And you allow and maintain that true opinion, combined with definition or rational explanation, is knowledge?

THEAETETUS: Exactly.

d *SOCRATES*: Then may we assume, Theaetetus, that today, and in this casual manner, we have found a truth which in former times many wise men have grown old and have not found?

THEAETETUS: At any rate, Socrates, I am satisfied with the present statement.

SOCRATES: Which is probably correct—for how can there be knowledge apart from definition and true opinion? And yet there is one point in what has been said which does not quite satisfy me.

THEAETETUS: What was it?

SOCRATES: What might seem to be the most ingenious notion of all: That
e the elements or letters are unknown, but the combination or syllables known.

THEAETETUS: And was that wrong?

SOCRATES: We shall soon know; for we have as hostages the instances which the author of the argument himself used.

THEAETETUS: What hostages?

SOCRATES: The letters, which are the elements; and the syllables, which are the combinations; he reasoned, did he not, from the letters of the alphabet?

THEAETETUS: Yes; he did.

203a *SOCRATES*: Let us take them and put them to the test, or rather, test ourselves: What was the way in which we learned letters? And, first of all, are we right in saying that syllables have a definition, but that letters have no definition?

THEAETETUS: I think so.

SOCRATES: I think so too; for, suppose that some one asks you to spell the first syllable of my name: Theaetetus, he says, what is SO?

THEAETETUS: I should reply S and O.

SOCRATES: That is the definition which you would give of the syllable?

THEAETETUS: I should.

b *SOCRATES*: I wish that you would give me a similar definition of the S.

THEAETETUS: But how can anyone, Socrates, tell the elements of an element? I can only reply, that S is a consonant, a mere noise, as of the tongue hissing; B, and most other letters, again, are neither vowel-sounds nor noises. Thus letters may be most truly said to be undefined; for even the most distinct of them, which are the seven vowels, have a sound only, but no definition at all.

SOCRATES: Then, I suppose, my friend, that we have been so far right in our idea about knowledge?

THEAETETUS: Yes; I think that we have.

SOCRATES: Well, but have we been right in maintaining that the syllables c
can be known, but not the letters?

THEAETETUS: I think so.

SOCRATES: And do we mean by a syllable two letters, or if there are more, all of them, or a single idea which arises out of the combination of them?

THEAETETUS: I should say that we mean all the letters.

SOCRATES: Take the case of the two letters S and O, which form the first syllable of my own name; must not he who knows the syllable, know both of them?

THEAETETUS: Certainly. d

SOCRATES: He knows, that is, the S and O?

THEAETETUS: Yes.

SOCRATES: But can he be ignorant of either singly and yet know both together?

THEAETETUS: Such a supposition, Socrates, is monstrous and unmeaning.

SOCRATES: But if he cannot know both without knowing each, then if he is ever to know the syllable, he must know the letters first; and thus the fine theory has again taken wings and departed.

THEAETETUS: Yes, with wonderful celerity. e

SOCRATES: Yes, we did not keep watch properly. Perhaps we ought to have maintained that a syllable is not the letters, but rather one single idea framed out of them, having a separate form distinct from them.

THEAETETUS: Very true; and a more likely notion than the other.

SOCRATES: Take care; let us not be cowards and betray a great and imposing theory.

THEAETETUS: No, indeed.

SOCRATES: Let us assume then, as we now say, that the syllable is a simple 204a
form arising out of the several combinations of harmonious elements—of letters or of any other elements.

THEAETETUS: Very good.

SOCRATES: And it must have no parts.

THEAETETUS: Why?

SOCRATES: Because that which has parts must be a whole of all the parts. Or would you say that a whole, although formed out of the parts, is a single notion different from all the parts?

THEAETETUS: I should.

b *SOCRATES*: And would you say that all and the whole are the same, or different?

THEAETETUS: I am not certain; but, as you like me to answer at once, I shall hazard the reply, that they are different.

SOCRATES: I approve of your readiness, Theaetetus, but I must take time to think whether I equally approve of your answer.

THEAETETUS: Yes; the answer is the point.

SOCRATES: According to this new view, the whole is supposed to differ from all?

THEAETETUS: Yes.

SOCRATES: Well, but is there any difference between all (in the plural) and the all (in the singular)? Take the case of number: When we say one,
c two, three, four, five, six; or when we say twice three, or three times two, or four and two, or three and two and one, are we speaking of the same or of different numbers?

THEAETETUS: Of the same.

SOCRATES: That is of six?

THEAETETUS: Yes.

SOCRATES: And in each form of expression we spoke of all the six?

THEAETETUS: True.

SOCRATES: Again, in speaking of all (in the plural) is there not one thing which we express?

THEAETETUS: Of course there is.

SOCRATES: And that is six?

THEAETETUS: Yes.

d *SOCRATES*: Then in predicating the word "all" of things measured by number, we predicate at the same time a singular and a plural?

THEAETETUS: Clearly we do.

SOCRATES: Again, the number of the acre and the acre are the same; are they not?

THEAETETUS: Yes.

SOCRATES: And the number of the stadium in like manner is the stadium?

THEAETETUS: Yes.

SOCRATES: And the army is the number of the army; and in all similar cases, the entire number of anything is the entire thing?

THEAETETUS: True.

e *SOCRATES*: And the number of each is the parts of each?

THEAETETUS: Exactly.

SOCRATES: Then as many things as have parts are made up of parts?

THEAETETUS: Clearly.

SOCRATES: But all the parts are admitted to be the all, if the entire number is the all?

THEAETETUS: True.

SOCRATES: Then the whole is not made up of parts, for it would be the all, if consisting of all the parts?

THEAETETUS: That is the inference.

SOCRATES: But is a part a part of anything but the whole?

THEAETETUS: Yes, of the all.

SOCRATES: You make a valiant defense, Theaetetus. And yet is not the all 205a
that of which nothing is wanting?

THEAETETUS: Certainly.

SOCRATES: And is not a whole likewise that from which nothing is absent? But that from which anything is absent is neither a whole nor all; if wanting in anything, both equally lose their entirety of nature.

THEAETETUS: I now think that there is no difference between a whole and all.

SOCRATES: But were we not saying that when a thing has parts, all the parts will be a whole and all?

THEAETETUS: Certainly.

SOCRATES: Then, as I was saying before, must not the alternative be that
either the syllable is not the letters, and then the letters are not parts b
of the syllable, or that the syllable will be the same with the letters, and will therefore be equally known with them?

THEAETETUS: You are right.

SOCRATES: And, in order to avoid this, we suppose it to be different from them?

THEAETETUS: Yes.

SOCRATES: But if letters are not parts of syllables, can you tell me of any other parts of syllables, which are not letters?

THEAETETUS: No, indeed, Socrates; for if I admit the existence of parts in a syllable, it would be ridiculous in me to give up letters and seek for other parts.

SOCRATES: Quite true, Theaetetus, and therefore, according to our present c
view, a syllable must surely be some indivisible form?

THEAETETUS: True.

SOCRATES: But do you remember, my friend, that only a little while ago we admitted and approved the statement, that of the first elements out of which all other things are compounded there could be no definition, because each of them when taken by itself is uncompounded; nor can one rightly attribute to them the words "being" or "this," because they are alien and inappropriate words, and for this reason the letters or elements were indefinable and unknown?

THEAETETUS: I remember.

d *SOCRATES*: And is not this also the reason why they are simple and indivisible? I can see no other.

THEAETETUS: No other reason can be given.

SOCRATES: Then is not the syllable in the same case as the elements or letters, if it has no parts and is one form?

THEAETETUS: To be sure.

SOCRATES: If, then, a syllable is a whole, and has many parts or letters, the letters as well as the syllable must be intelligible and expressible, since all the parts are acknowledged to be the same as the whole?

e *THEAETETUS*: True.

SOCRATES: But if it be one and indivisible, then the syllables and the letters are alike undefined and unknown, and for the same reason?

THEAETETUS: I cannot deny that.

SOCRATES: We cannot, therefore, agree in the opinion of him who says that the syllable can be known and expressed, but not the letters.

THEAETETUS: Certainly not; if we may trust the argument.

206a *SOCRATES*: Well, but will you not be equally inclined to disagree with him, when you remember your own experience in learning to read?

THEAETETUS: What experience?

SOCRATES: Why, that in learning you were kept trying to distinguish the separate letters both by the eye and by the ear, in order that, when you heard them spoken or saw them written, you might not be confused by their position.

THEAETETUS: Very true.

SOCRATES: And is the education of the harp-player complete unless he can
b tell what string answers to a particular note; the notes, as every one would allow, are the elements or letters of music?

THEAETETUS: Exactly.

SOCRATES: Then, if we argue from the letters and syllables which we know to other simples and compounds, we shall say that the letters or simple elements as a class are much more certainly known than the syllables, and much more indispensable to a perfect knowledge of any subject; and if some one says that the syllable is known and the letter unknown, we shall consider that either intentionally or unintentionally he is talking nonsense?

THEAETETUS: Exactly.

SOCRATES: And there might be given other proofs of this belief, if I am not c
mistaken. But do not let us in looking for them lose sight of the question before us, which is the meaning of the statement, that right opinion with rational definition or explanation is the most perfect form of knowledge.

THEAETETUS: We must not.

SOCRATES: Well, and what is the meaning of the term "explanation"? I think that we have a choice of three meanings.

THEAETETUS: What are they?

SOCRATES: In the first place, the meaning may be, manifesting one's d
thought by the voice with verbs and nouns, imaging an opinion in the stream which flows from the lips, as in a mirror or water. Does not explanation appear to be of this nature?

THEAETETUS: Certainly; he who so manifests his thought, is said to explain himself.

SOCRATES: And every one who is not born deaf or dumb is able sooner or later to manifest what he thinks of anything; and if so, all those who have
a right opinion about anything will also have right explanation; nor will e
right opinion be anywhere found to exist apart from knowledge.

THEAETETUS: True.

SOCRATES: Let us not, therefore, hastily charge him who gave this account of knowledge with uttering an unmeaning word; for perhaps he only intended to say, that when a person was asked what was the nature of
anything, he should be able to answer his questioner by giving the ele- 207a
ments of the thing.

THEAETETUS: As for example, Socrates . . . ?

SOCRATES: As, for example, when Hesiod says that a waggon is made up of a hundred planks. Now, neither you nor I could describe all of them individually; but if anyone asked what is a waggon, we should be content to answer, that a waggon consists of wheels, axle, body, rims, yoke.

THEAETETUS: Certainly.

SOCRATES: And our opponent will probably laugh at us, just as he would if
we professed to be grammarians and to give a grammatical account b
of the name of Theaetetus, and yet could only tell the syllables and not the letters of your name—that would be true opinion, and not knowledge; for knowledge, as has been already remarked, is not attained until, combined with true opinion, there is an enumeration of the elements out of which anything is composed.

THEAETETUS: Yes.

SOCRATES: In the same general way, we might also have true opinion about
a waggon; but he who can describe its essence by an enumeration of
c the hundred planks, adds rational explanation to true opinion, and
instead of opinion has art and knowledge of the nature of a waggon,
in that he attains to the whole through the elements.

THEAETETUS: And do you not agree in that view, Socrates?

SOCRATES: If you do, my friend; but I want to know first, whether you admit
the resolution of all things into their elements to be a rational explanation of them, and the consideration of them in syllables or larger
d combinations of them to be irrational—is this your view?

THEAETETUS: Precisely.

SOCRATES: Well, and do you conceive that a man has knowledge of any element who at one time affirms and at another time denies that element of something, or thinks that the same thing is composed of different elements at different times?

THEAETETUS: Assuredly not.

SOCRATES: And do you not remember that in your case and in that of others this often occurred in the process of learning to read?

e *THEAETETUS*: You mean that I mistook the letters and misspelt the syllables?

SOCRATES: Yes.

THEAETETUS: To be sure; I perfectly remember, and I am very far from supposing that they who are in this condition have knowledge.

SOCRATES: When a person at the time of learning writes the name of Theaetetus, and thinks that he ought to write and does write Th and e; but,
208a again, meaning to write the name of Theododorus, thinks that he
ought to write and does write T and e—can we suppose that he knows
the first syllables of your two names?

THEAETETUS: We have already admitted that such a one has not yet attained knowledge.

SOCRATES: And in like manner be may enumerate without knowing them the second and third and fourth syllables of your name?

THEAETETUS: He may.

SOCRATES: And in that case, when he knows the order of the letters and can write them out correctly, he has right opinion?

THEAETETUS: Clearly.

b *SOCRATES*: But although we admit that he has right opinion, he will still be
without knowledge?

THEAETETUS: Yes.

SOCRATES: And yet he will have explanation, as well as right opinion, for he knew the order of the letters when he wrote; and this we admit to be explanation.

THEAETETUS: True.

SOCRATES: Then, my friend, there is such a thing as right opinion united with definition or explanation, which does not as yet attain to the exactness of knowledge.

THEAETETUS: It would seem so.

SOCRATES: And what we fancied to be a perfect definition of knowledge is a dream only. But perhaps we had better not say so as yet, for were there not three explanations of knowledge, one of which must, as we
said, be adopted by him who maintains knowledge to be true opinion c
combined with rational explanation? And very likely there may be found some one who will not prefer this but the third.

THEAETETUS: You are quite right; there is still one remaining. The first was the image or expression of the mind in speech; the second, which has just been mentioned, is a way of reaching the whole by an enumeration of the elements. But what is the third definition?

SOCRATES: There is, further, the popular notion of telling the mark or sign of difference which distinguishes the thing in question from all others.

THEAETETUS: Can you give me any example of such a definition?

SOCRATES: As, for example, in the case of the sun, I think that you would d
be contented with the statement that the sun is the brightest of the heavenly bodies which revolve about the earth.

THEAETETUS: Certainly.

SOCRATES: Understand why: the reason is, as I was just now saying, that if you get at the difference and distinguishing characteristic of each thing, then, as many persons affirm, you will get at the definition or explanation of it; but while you lay hold only of the common and not of the characteristic notion, you will only have the definition of those things to which this common quality belongs.

THEAETETUS: I understand you, and your account of definition is in my e
judgment correct.

SOCRATES: But he, who having right opinion about anything, can find out the difference which distinguishes it from other things will know that of which before he had only an opinion.

THEAETETUS: Yes; that is what we are maintaining.

Socrates: Nevertheless, Theaetetus, on a nearer view, I find myself quite disappointed; the picture, which at a distance was not so bad, has now become altogether unintelligible.

Theaetetus: What do you mean?

209a *Socrates*: I will endeavor to explain: I will suppose myself to have true opinion of you, and if to this I add your definition, then I have knowledge, but if not, opinion only.

Theaetetus: Yes.

Socrates: The definition was assumed to be the interpretation of your difference.

Theaetetus: True.

Socrates: But when I had only opinion, I had no conception of your distinguishing characteristics.

Theaetetus: I suppose not.

Socrates: Then I must have conceived of some general or common nature which no more belonged to you than to another.

b *Theaetetus*: True.

Socrates: Tell me, now—How in that case could I have formed a judgment of you any more than of anyone else? Suppose that I imagine Theaetetus to be a man who has nose, eyes, and mouth, and every other member complete; how would that enable me to distinguish Theaetetus from Theodorus, or from some outer barbarian?

Theaetetus: How could it?

c *Socrates*: Or if I had further conceived of you, not only as having nose and eyes, but as having a snub nose and prominent eyes, should I have any more notion of you than of myself and others who resemble me?

Theaetetus: Certainly not.

Socrates: Surely I can have no conception of Theaetetus until your snubnosedness has left an impression on my mind different from the snubnosedness of all others whom I have ever seen, and until your other peculiarities have a like distinctness; and so when I meet you tomorrow the right opinion will be re-called?

Theaetetus: Most true.

d *Socrates*: Then right opinion implies the perception of differences?

Theaetetus: Clearly.

Socrates: What, then, shall we say of adding reason or explanation to right opinion? If the meaning is, that we should form an opinion of the way in which something differs from another thing, the proposal is ridiculous.

Theaetetus: How so?

Socrates: We are supposed to acquire a right opinion of the differences which distinguish one thing from another when we have already a right opinion of them, and so we go round and round: the revolution e
of the scytal, or pestle, or any other rotatory machine, in the same circles, is as nothing compared with such a requirement; and we may be truly described as the blind directing the blind; for to add those things which we already have, in order that we may learn what we already think, is like a soul utterly benighted.

Theaetetus: Tell me; what were you going to say just now, when you asked the question?

Socrates: If, my boy, the argument, in speaking of adding the definition, had used the word to "know," and not merely "have an opinion" of the difference, this which is the most promising of all the definitions of knowledge would have come to a pretty end, for to know is surely to 210a
acquire knowledge.

Theaetetus: True.

Socrates: And so, when the question is asked, What is knowledge? This fair argument will answer "Right opinion with knowledge"—knowledge, that is, of difference, for this, as the said argument maintains, is adding the definition.

Theaetetus: That seems to be true.

Socrates: But how utterly foolish, when we are asking what is knowledge, that the reply should only be, right opinion with knowledge of difference or of anything! And so, Theaetetus, knowledge is neither sensation nor true opinion, nor yet definition and explanation accom- b
panying and added to true opinion?

Theaetetus: I suppose not.

Socrates: And are you still in labor and travail, my dear friend, or have you brought all that you have to say about knowledge to the birth?

Theaetetus: I am sure, Socrates, that you have elicited from me a good deal more than ever was in me.

Socrates: And does not my art show that you have brought forth wind, and that the offspring of your brain are not worth bringing up?

Theaetetus: Very true.

Socrates: But if, Theaetetus, you should ever conceive afresh, you will c
be all the better for the present investigation, and if not, you will be soberer and humbler and gentler to other men, and will be too modest to fancy that you know what you do not know. These are the limits

of my art; I can no further go, nor do I know aught of the things which
great and famous men know or have known in this or former ages. The
office of a midwife I, like my mother, have received from God; she
d delivered women, I deliver men; but they must be young and noble
and fair.

And now I have to go to the porch of the King Archon, where I am to meet Meletus and his indictment. Tomorrow morning, Theodorus, I shall hope to see you again at this place.

ENDNOTES

INTRODUCTION

[1] Jaspers, Karl. *Socrates, Buddha, Confucius, Jesus: The Paradigmatic Individuals.* Trans. Ralph Mannheim. New York: Harcourt Brace Jovanovich, Publishers, 1962, p. 6.
[2] Emerson, Ralph Waldo. "Plato; Or, The Philosopher." *The Complete Essays and Other Writings of Ralph Waldo Emerson.* New York: The Modern Library, 1950, pp. 471–2.
[3] Plato, *The Republic of Plato.* Trans. Allan Bloom. New York: Basic Books, Inc., Publishers, 1968, 485a–486a.
[4] Nietzsche, Friedrich. *Ecce Homo.* Trans. Anthony M. Ludovici. New York: Barnes and Noble, Inc., 2006, p. 96 and p. 94.
[5] See especially chapter 4 of Mitchell Miller's *Plato's "Parmenides": The Conversion of the Soul.* Princeton, NJ: Princeton University Press, 1986.

MENO

[1] Cf. Arist. *Pol.* i. 13, § 10.
[2] Cf. *Theaetetus* 146 D.
[3] Cf. Aristot. *Post. Anal.* I i. 6.
[4] Or: whether a certain area is capable of being inscribed as a triangle in a certain circle.
[5] Or: when you apply it to the given line, i.e., the diameter of the circle (αὐτοῦ).
[6] Or: similar to the area so applied.
[7] Theog. 33 ff.
[8] *Ibid.* 435 ff.
[9] Cf. *Euthyphro* 11b.

SUGGESTED READING

CHAPPELL, T. D. J. *Reading Plato's "Theaetetus."* USA: Hackett Publishing Company, Inc., 2005.

CORNFORD, F. M. *Plato's Theory of Knowledge: The "Theaetetus" and "Sophist" of Plato, Translated and with an Introduction and Running Commentary.* London: Routledge and Kegan Paul, 1979.

FRIEDLÄNDER, PAUL. *Plato: An Introduction.* Trans. Hans Meyerhoff. New York: Pantheon Books, Inc., 1958.

GRUBE, G. M. A. *Plato's Thought.* London: Methuen & Co., 1935.

GUTHRIE, W. K. C. *A History of Greek Philosophy, Vol. IV: Plato: The Man and His Dialogues: Earlier Period.* Great Britain: Cambridge University Press, 1995.

———. *A History of Greek Philosophy, Vol. V: The Later Plato and the Academy.* Great Britain: Cambridge University Press, 1995.

HEIDEGGER, MARTIN. "Plato's Doctrine of Truth." Trans. Thomas Sheehan. *Pathmarks.* New York: Cambridge University Press, 1998.

KAHN, CHARLES H. *Plato and the Socratic Dialogue: The Philosophical Use of a Literary Form.* New York: Cambridge University Press, 1998.

MILLER, MITCHELL H. *Plato's "Parmenides": The Conversion of the Soul.* Princeton, NJ: Princeton University Press, 1986.

NEHAMAS, ALEXANDER. *The Art of Living: Socratic Reflections from Plato to Foucault.* Berkeley and Los Angeles, CA: University of California Press, 1998.

VLASTOS, GREGORY. *Socrates: Ironist and Moral Philosopher.* New York: Cambridge University Press, 1991.

———. *Platonic Studies.* Princeton, NJ: Princeton University Press, 1981.

Look for the following titles, available now from The Barnes & Noble Library of Essential Reading.

Visit your Barnes & Noble bookstore, or shop online at *www.bn.com/loer*

NONFICTION

Age of Reason, The	Thomas Paine	0760778957
Age of Revolution, The	Winston S. Churchill	0760768595
Alexander	Theodore Ayrault Dodge	0760773491
American Indian Stories	Zitkala-Ša	0760765502
Ancient Greek Historians, The	J. B. Bury	0760776350
Annals of Imperial Rome, The	Tacitus	0760788898
Antichrist, The	Friedrich Nietzsche	0760777705
Autobiography of Benjamin Franklin, The	Benjamin Franklin	0760768617
Autobiography of Charles Darwin, The	Charles Darwin	0760769087
Babylonian Life and History	E. A. Wallis Budge	0760765499
Beyond the Pleasure Principle	Sigmund Freud	0760774919
Birth of Britain, The	Winston S. Churchill	0760768579
Birth of Tragedy, The	Friedrich Nietzsche	0760780862
Century of Dishonor, A	Helen Hunt Jackson	0760778973
Characters and Events of Roman History	Guglielmo Ferrero	0760765928
Chemical History of a Candle, The	Michael Faraday	0760765227
City of God, The	Saint Augustine	0760779023
Civil War, The	Julius Caesar	0760768943
Common Law, The	Oliver Wendell Holmes	0760754985
Confessions	Jean-Jacques Rousseau	0760773599
Conquest of Gaul, The	Julius Caesar	0760768951

Consolation of Philosophy, The	Boethius	0760769796
Conversations with Socrates	Xenophon	0760770441
Creative Evolution	Henri Bergson	0760765480
Critique of Judgment	Immanuel Kant	0760762023
Critique of Practical Reason	Immanuel Kant	0760760942
Critique of Pure Reason	Immanuel Kant	0760755949
Dark Night of the Soul, The	St. John of the Cross	0760765871
De Anima	Aristotle	0760780773
Democracy and Education	John Dewey	0760765863
Democracy in America	Alexis de Tocqueville	0760752303
Descent of Man and Selection in Relation to Sex, The	Charles Darwin	0760763119
Dialogues concerning Natural Religion	David Hume	0760777713
Diary from Dixie, A	Mary Boykin Chesnut	0760779031
Discourse on Method	René Descartes	0760756023
Discourses on Livy	Niccolò Machiavelli	0760771731
Dolorous Passion of Our Lord Jesus Christ, The	Anne Catherine Emmerich	0760771715
Early History of Rome, The	Titus Livy	0760770239
Ecce Homo	Friedrich Nietzsche	0760777721
Egyptian Book of the Dead, The	E. A. Wallis Budge	0760768382
Elements, The	Euclid	0760763127
Emile	Jean-Jacques Rousseau	0760773513
Encheiridion	Epictetus	0760770204
Enquiry concerning Human Understanding, An	David Hume	0760755922
Essay Concerning Human Understanding, An	John Locke	0760760497
Essays, The	Francis Bacon	0760770182
Essence of Christianity, The	Ludwig Feuerbach	076075764X
Ethics and On the Improvement of the Understanding	Benedict de Spinoza	0760768374
Evidence as to Man's Place in Nature	Thomas H. Huxley	0760783381
Evolution and Ethics	Thomas H. Huxley	0760783373
Expression of the Emotions in Man and Animals, The	Charles Darwin	0760780803
Extraordinary Popular Delusions and the Madness of Crowds	Charles Mackay	0760755825
Fall of Troy, The	Quintus of Smyrna	0760768366
Fifteen Decisive Battles of the Western World	Edward Shepherd Creasy	0760754950
Florentine History	Niccolò Machiavelli	0760756015

From Manassas to Appomattox	James Longstreet	0760759200
Great Democracies, The	Winston S. Churchill	0760768609
Guide for the Perplexed, The	Moses Maimonides	0760757577
Hannibal	Theodore Ayrault Dodge	076076896X
Happy Hunting-Grounds, The	Kermit Roosevelt	0760755817
History of the Conquest of Mexico, The	William H. Prescott	0760759227
History of the Conquest of Peru, The	William H. Prescott	076076137X
History of the Donner Party, The	Charles F. McGlashan	0760752427
How the Other Half Lives	Jacob A. Riis	0760755892
How We Think	John Dewey	0760770387
Hunting the Grisly and Other Sketches	Theodore Roosevelt	0760752338
Imitation of Christ, The	Thomas À. Kempis	0760755914
In His Steps	Charles M. Sheldon	0760755779
Influence of Sea Power upon History, The, 1660–1783	Alfred Thayer Mahan	0760754993
Interesting Narrative of the Life of Olaudah Equiano, The	Olaudah Equiano	0760773505
Interior Castle, The	St. Teresa of Avila	0760770247
Introduction to Logic	Immanuel Kant	0760770409
Introduction to Mathematical Philosophy	Bertrand Russell	0760773408
Introduction to Mathematics	Alfred North Whitehead	076076588X
Kama Sutra and Ananga Ranga	Sir Richard Francis Burton	076077899X
Kingdom of God is Within You, The	Leo Tolstoy	0760765529
Lady's Life in the Rockies, A	Isabella Bird	0760763135
Letters and Saying of Epicurus	Epicurus	0760763283
Leviathan, The	Thomas Hobbes	0760755930
Life of General Nathan Bedford, The	John Allan Wyeth	0760780196
Life of Johnson	James Boswell	0760773483
Lives of the Caesars, The	Suetonius	0760757585
Meditations	Marcus Aurelius	076075229X
Memoirs	William T. Sherman	0760773688
Metaphysics	Aristotle	0760773637
Montcalm and Wolfe	Francis Parkman	0760768358
Montessori Method, The	Maria Montessori	0760749957
Mosby's Memoirs	John Singleton Mosby	0760773726
Napoleon's Art of War	George C. D'Aguilar	0760773564
New World, The	Winston S. Churchill	0760768587
Nicomachean Ethics	Aristotle	0760752362
Notes on Nursing	Florence Nightingale	0760749949
On Liberty	John Stuart Mill	0760755000

On the Genealogy of Morals	Friedrich Nietzsche	0760780811
On War	Carl von Clausewitz	0760755973
Oregon Trail, The	Francis Parkman	076075232X
Orthodoxy	G. K. Chesterton	0760786313
Outline of History, The: Volume 1	H. G. Wells	0760758662
Outline of History, The: Volume 2	H. G. Wells	0760758670
Passing of the Armies, The	Joshua L. Chamberlain	0760760527
Personal Memoirs of P. H. Sheridan	Philip H. Sheridan	0760773750
Personal Memoirs of U. S. Grant	Ulysses S. Grant	0760749906
Philosophy of Art	G. W. F. Hegel	0760783225
Philosophy of Friedrich Nietzsche, The	H. L. Mencken	0760780919
Philosophy of History, The	G. W. F. Hegel	0760757631
Plutarch's Lives: Volume 1	Plutarch	0760780927
Plutarch's Lives: Volume 2	Plutarch	0760780935
Political Economy for Beginners	Millicent Garrett Fawcett	0760754977
Politics	Aristotle	0760768935
Poor Richard's Almanack	Benjamin Franklin	0760762015
Pragmatism	William James	0760749965
Praise of Folly, The	Desiderius Erasmus	0760757607
Principia Ethica	G. E. Moore	0760765464
Problems of Philosophy, The	Bertrand Russell	076075604X
Prolegomena to Any Future Metaphysics	Immanuel Kant	0760786321
Recollections and Letters	Robert E. Lee	0760759197
Relativity	Albert Einstein	0760759219
Rights of Man, The	Thomas Paine	0760755019
Rough Riders, The	Theodore Roosevelt	0760755760
Science and Method	Henri Poincare	0760755868
Second Treatise of Government, The	John Locke	0760760950
Sense of Beauty, The	George Santayana	0760770425
Shakespearean Tragedy	A. C. Bradley	0760771693
Social Contract, The	Jean-Jacques Rousseau	0760770212
Stonewall Jackson and the American Civil War	G. F. R. Henderson	0760779546
Subjection of Women, The	John Stuart Mill	076077174X
Theory of Moral Sentiments, The	Adam Smith	0760758689
Timaeus & Critias	Plato	0760780854
Totem and Taboo	Sigmund Freud	0760765200
Tractatus Logico-Philosophicus	Ludwig Wittgenstein	0760752354
Tragic Sense of Life	Miguel de Unamuno	0760777764
Travels of Marco Polo, The	Marco Polo	0760765898
Treatise Concerning the Principles of Human Knowledge, A	George Berkeley	0760777691

Treatise of Human Nature, A	David Hume	0760771723
Trial and Death of Socrates, The	Plato	0760762007
Twelve Years a Slave	Solomon Northup	0760783349
Up From Slavery	Booker T. Washington	0760752346
Utilitarianism	John Stuart Mill	0760771758
Vindication of the Rights of Woman, A	Mary Wollstonecraft	0760754942
Voyage of the *Beagle*, The	Charles Darwin	0760754969
Wealth of Nations, The	Adam Smith	0760757615
Wilderness Hunter, The	Theodore Roosevelt	0760756031
Will to Believe and Human Immortality, The	William James	0760770190
Will to Power, The	Friedrich Nietzsche	0760777772
Worst Journey in the World, The	Aspley Cherry-Garrard	0760757593

FICTION AND LITERATURE

Abbott, Edwin A.	Flatland	0760755876
Austen, Jane	Love and Freindship	0760768560
Braddon, Mary Elizabeth	Lady Audley's Secret	0760763046
Bronte, Charlotte	Professor, The	0760768854
Burroughs, Edgar Rice	Land that Time Forgot, The	0760768862
Burroughs, Edgar Rice	Martian Tales Trilogy, The	076075585X
Butler, Samuel	Way of All Flesh, The	0760765855
Castiglione, Baldesar	Book of the Courtier, The	0760768323
Cather, Willa	Alexander's Bridge	0760768870
Cather, Willa	One of Ours	0760777683
Chaucer, Geoffrey	Troilus and Criseyde	0760768919
Chesterton, G. K.	Ball and the Cross, The	0760783284
Chesterton, G. K.	Innocence and Wisdom of Father Brown, The	0760773556
Chesterton, G. K.	Man Who Was Thursday, The	0760763100
Childers, Erskine	Riddle of the Sands, The	0760765235
Cleland, John	Fanny Hill	076076591X
Conrad, Joseph	Secret Agent, The	0760783217
Cooper, James Fenimore	Pioneers, The	0760779015
Cummings, E. E.	Enormous Room, The	076077904X
Defoe, Daniel	Journal of the Plague Year, A	0760752370
Dos Passos, John	Three Soldiers	0760757542
Doyle, Arthur Conan	Complete Brigadier Gerard, The	0760768897
Doyle, Arthur Conan	Lost World, The	0760755833
Doyle, Arthur Conan	White Company and Sir Nigel, The	0760768900

Eddison, E. R.	Worm Oroborus, The	0760773645
Fitzgerald, F. Scott	Collected Stories of F. Scott Fitzgerald	0760786305
Forster, E. M.	Where Angels Fear to Tread	076078325X
Gaskell, Elizabeth	Cranford	0760795983
Gilman, Charlotte Perkins	Herland and The Yellow Wallpaper	0760777667
Goethe, Johann Wolfgang von	Sorrows of Young Werther, The	0760768331
Goldsmith, Oliver	Vicar of Wakefield, The	0760783292
Grey, Zane	Riders of the Purple Sage	0760757550
Guest, Charlotte E. (tr.)	Mabinogion, The	0760771707
Hamsun, Knut	Hunger	0760780870
Hazlitt, William Carew	Shakespeare's Jest Books	0760783330
Huxley, Aldous	Crome Yellow	0760760500
James, Henry	American, The	0760773653
Jerome, Jerome K.	Three Men in a Boat	0760757569
Lamb, Charles and Mary	Tales from Shakespeare	0760780846
Lawrence, D. H.	Lost Girl, The	0760773319
Masters, Edgar Lee	Spoon River Anthology	0760791058
Maugham, W. Somerset	Three Early Novels	0760768625
Melville, Herman	Bartleby the Scrivener and The Confidence Man	0760777640
Melville, Herman	Israel Potter	076077773X
Millay, Edna St. Vincent	Early Works of Edna St. Vincent	0760780781
Morley, Christopher	Haunted Bookshop, The	0760783454
Munro, H. H.	Complete Works of Saki, The	0760773734
Norris, Frank	McTeague	0760773742
Rabelais, Francois	Gargantua and Pantagruel	0760763143
Radcliffe, Ann	Mysteries of Udolpho, The	0760763151
Sabatini, Rafael	Captain Blood	0760755965
Sacher-Masoch, Leopold von	Venus in Furs	0760763089
Sade, Marquis de	Justine	0760768978
Schreiner, Olive	Story of an African Farm, The	0760773521
Sienkiewicz, Henrik	Quo Vadis	0760763097
Somerville, Edith, and Martin Ross	Some Experiences of an Irish R.M.	0760765804
Sterne, Laurence	Life and Opinions of Tristram Shandy, Gentleman, The	0760763054
Stevenson, Robert Louis	Black Arrow, The	0760773602
Swift, Jonathan	Modest Proposal and Other Satires, A	0760760519
Tolstoy, Leo	Hadji Murád	076077353X

THE BARNES & NOBLE
LIBRARY OF ESSENTIAL READING

This series has been established to provide affordable access to books of literary, academic, and historic value—works of both well-known writers and those who deserve to be rediscovered. Selected and introduced by scholars and specialists with an intimate knowledge of the works, these volumes present complete, original texts in a modern, readable typeface—welcoming a new generation of readers to influential and important books of the past. With more than 300 titles already in print and more than 100 forthcoming, the Library of Essential Reading offers an unrivaled variety of thought, scholarship, and entertainment. Best of all, these handsome and durable paperbacks are priced to be exceptionally affordable. For a full list of titles, visit *www.bn.com/loer.*